Fifty Years in the Doghouse

Fifty Years in the Doghouse

BY

LLOYD ALEXANDER

G. P. PUTNAM'S SONS
NEW YORK

For William Mapel, who thought of it first, and who named it.

L. A.

Author's Note

T HE American Society for the Prevention of Cruelty to Animals has another branch of operations: Kindness to Authors, which provides everything an author could want in the way of cooperation and encouragement. Bill Ryan is a man not only of infinite resource but also of patience. From his own literary experience, the Society's Administrative Vice-President, William Mapel, has developed a special intuition about another author's needs.

My thanks, also, must go to William Rockefeller, the Society's President, and to the divisional directors: Arthur L. Amundsen, ASPCA Operations; Colonel Edmond M. Rowan, Humane Work; Mrs. George Fielding Eliot, Publications and Programs; Dr. John E. Whitehead, Hospital and Clinic; Thomas A. Fegan, Comptroller; and a particular note of gratitude to Jay Beyersdorf and Janice Paprin.

For them, nothing has been too much trouble, nothing has demanded too much time.

To them, and to all the Society staff, active and retired, who willingly shared their knowledge and experience with me, I should like to express my sincerest appreciation.

L.A.

Contents

Fifty Years in the Doghouse

1

Is There a Toad in Your Cornerstone?

IF an elephant ever decided to reveal the whereabouts of
the Elephants' Graveyard, he would tell his secret to a man
named William Michael Ryan, of the American Society for
the Prevention of Cruelty to Animals.

Big, blue-eyed, white-haired, with a deft pair of hands and
a smile that looks three feet wide, Ryan knows pretty much
all there is to know about making friends with animals. Perhaps this is a special blessing of the Irish.

Whatever the gift, Ryan has been an ASPCA special agent
for fifty years—the longest anyone has served continuously
with the Society since its founding in 1866. From ASPCA
headquarters in New York City, as one of the organization's
seventeen uniformed agents, Ryan has coped with something
like half a million beasts, birds and reptiles. Most of them
were in trouble. Getting them out has been a matter of life
or death: the animals'—and sometimes Ryan's.

From what Ryan has seen, the animals are still trying to
figure us out. Although the animals generally like us personally, they haven't entirely come to terms with our gadg-
ets, architecture and other handiwork. A cat sometimes
mistakes a chimney for a brick-lined mousehole and gets
trapped in it. Rush-hour traffic can drive a dog to despair. A

13

horse finds himself unintentionally in somebody's living room. Chimpanzees wake up in boardinghouse beds. A bull suddenly materializes in a powder room. Lions with no pressing engagements may stroll through Manhattan.

The situations are not always that grave. In some cases, a human, not an animal, presents the larger problem. One busy afternoon, a carpenter working on a new building in the East Fifties phoned Ryan to advise about a cornerstone-laying ceremony.

"Listen," the carpenter said, "these people are plastering up a toad in that cornerstone. I know it's only a toad and all that. But I mean, what the hell—it doesn't seem right. And the toad sure doesn't like it!"

This was Ryan's first call involving a toad. Nevertheless, a toad, as far as Ryan and the ASPCA were concerned, rated as much consideration as any other creature.

"Stay there," Ryan told the carpenter. "I'm on my way."

Ryan drove through traffic with a dispatch a cabbie would have envied. He found the carpenter waiting at the corner. The new building, the carpenter explained, belonged to Madame Charmaine, a famous Parisian fashion designer. As the carpenter had heard, Madame Charmaine believed the susperstition that a toad in a cornerstone brings good luck. She now intended putting it to the test.

Ryan headed for the front of the building and made his way through the crowd of well-wishers. The guests of honor, Ryan discovered later, included the French Consul General and several other dignitaries. Madame Charmaine, in one of her newest creations, waved a silver trowel.

Ryan stands a little under six feet, but when an animal is in any kind of danger he seems about eight feet four. The policeman-style cap, dark uniform and pistol on his hip may account for some of this impressiveness, although Ryan would look impressive walking around wearing a barrel.

He stopped before Madame Charmaine and, in a calm,

patient voice, as if he had asked the same question a thousand times before, he said, "Madam, is there a toad in your cornerstone?"

Madame Charmaine was as noted for her Gallic temperament as for her fashions. When she finally calmed down enough to speak English, she demanded to know whose affair it was, this toad! What Madame Charmaine chose to put in her cornerstone concerned no one but Madame Charmaine herself.

Ryan admitted this was generally true. In the pure accent of New York, he tried to convey to the excited Frenchwoman that walling up a live toad could be reasonably construed as cruelty. Under New York State law, Ryan is empowered to act in such cases. Ryan has his own Irish temper and vocabulary which he uses when he has to; much of the time, he relies on a touch of blarney. It usually works as well on humans as it does on animals. It did not work with Madame Charmaine.

"You will do me the favor to get out," she cried. "Leave! *Immédiatement!*"

Unruffled, Ryan tipped his cap politely. "See you in court," he said.

By this time a dark-suited, gray-haired man had come up beside Madame Charmaine. He was, it turned out, one of her lawyers. He called Ryan back: "Listen, officer, this is a joke, isn't it?"

Ryan assured him he was quite serious. He also pointed out that if Madame Charmaine went ahead with her cornerstone and the builders went ahead with their building, the fashion designer might find herself obliged to tear down several walls. It would be easier to remove the toad now while the removing was good.

The lawyer whispered hurriedly in Madame Charmaine's ear. With a furious glance at Ryan, the fashion designer uncapped the cornerstone and brought out the prisoner.

Ryan had been expecting a garden toad. What emerged was the biggest Texas horned toad he had ever seen.

"All right," said the lawyer, "he's out. Now what do you want?"

Ryan offered to take the former captive back to one of the ASPCA shelters. The six in New York City have housed everything from three-day-old kittens to full-grown lions, and a horned toad, even a Texas one, would hardly have caused a stir. Wild animals usually get returned to their natural environments; but others are available for adoption and Ryan felt sure someone in Manhattan would be looking for a horned toad.

This seemed plausible to the lawyer. Madame Charmaine took a different view.

"*Eh bien,* that toad still belongs to me," she said angrily. "He is my property. I do not have to give him to anybody."

Ryan agreed. Madame Charmaine had every right to keep the toad—as long as she looked after it properly. The only question was: did Madame Charmaine have the kind of facilities a toad would enjoy? If not, she might still be charged with cruelty.

"Go away!" Madame Charmaine shouted. "I do what I want with my toad! *C'est ridicule!*"

"I think," said the lawyer, "we'd better talk this over."

Still fuming, Madame Charmaine led the lawyer and Ryan to her original building a few doors down the street and ushered them into her office. Hardly in a frame of mind to play the gracious hostess, Madame Charmaine put the toad on her desk.

A horned toad looks like one of Nature's practical jokes. It has the color of sand and rock; its edges are fringed, as if a dressmaker had trimmed it out with pinking shears. Spiky scales run down its back, and horns jut from its head. But none of this exists for amusement. The horns discourage snakes from swallowing the toad and are thus an important accessory as far as the toad is concerned. With its fringed edges, the toad can dig itself quickly into the sand, using a kind of back-beat double-shuffle not unlike certain modern dances. The color is excellent camouflage.

The toad was considerably more functional than most of Madame Charmaine's fabrications—and Madame Charmaine recognized good design when she saw it.

"You know," Madame Charmaine said, "he is very interesting, this toad. He is very well arranged."

"Wouldn't you say he deserved a better break than being suffocated in your cornerstone?" Ryan asked.

When frightened, horned toads play dead. This one had been doing so ever since Madame Charmaine had released him. Now he ventured to open an eye and glance wearily about him.

"*Tiens*, he winked at me!" said Madame Charmaine delightedly. "He is an agreeable one." She looked at the toad again. "*Non*," she added, "it would not be just to lock him in the cornerstone. He is mine and he will stay with me."

That was all very well, Ryan said. But a toad wasn't a mechanical toy. It had to have a place to live and it had to eat.

Madame Charmaine raised an eyebrow. The toad's menu had never occurred to her. "What does he eat?" she asked Ryan.

"Oh, grubs and things, mealworms probably," Ryan said.

Madame Charmaine's expression changed and she gave a shudder. "Worms?"

"What do you expect him to eat?" Ryan asked. "Crêpes Suzette?"

"Do you wish to say then," Madame Charmaine cried, "that I must search New York for worms?"

"You might get by on hamburger," Ryan said.

"Toads!" Madame Charmaine said in despair. "Why must they be so complicated?"

"He was doing fine in Texas," Ryan said.

Madame Charmaine thought for a while. *"Eh bien,"* she said, "if he must have the worms, he will have them."

The lawyer looked much relieved. Everyone shook hands all around. "Tell me, just between us," the lawyer said to Ryan. "Madame Charmaine's going to keep this toad and she's going to look after it. I don't know why, but she's taken a liking to it. So everything's all right, as far as that goes. But what I want to know is this: if she hadn't gone along with you—just suppose she'd plastered up that cornerstone— would you really have made her take the building apart?"

The ASPCA agent grinned at him. Ryan, when he wants to convey important or confidential information, has a way of tilting his head to one side and lowering his voice. He drew a little closer to the lawyer. "Damned right I would have," he said.

As Ryan was about to leave the office, Madame Charmaine stopped him. *"Monsieur,"* she said, "you are a most unusual man. In all this affair about a toad, I look at him and I see him for the first time. I see he is a gorgeous toad, more clever than anything even I could do. And I think, yes, this man is right. So, if this little animal is important to him, it must be important to me, too."

The last Ryan heard was that Madame Charmaine had in- stalled the toad in her penthouse, in a sunny, pebbled gar- den. It was a more exotic atmosphere than Texas, but the toad seemed to be enjoying it; which, as far as Ryan was concerned, was all that counted.

Another of Ryan's cases brought him even closer to taking a building apart. It concerned a horse, not a toad. The horse was not in a cornerstone but in a situation no less compli- cated: under a flight of steps.

A few years ago, when horse-drawn vehicles were more common in Manhattan than they are now, a deliveryman's horse bolted. No one knew exactly what had frightened the animal in the first place. Whatever it was, the horse must have felt he would be better off under cover. After galloping down the street, kicking the wagon to pieces as if it had been a matchbox and breaking loose from his harness, the horse found sanctuary under the stairwell of one of the old brownstone houses.

Police called Ryan to the scene because more ingenuity was involved than simply leading the horse out again. The landlady, who lived in a basement apartment, stored empty rubbish cans under the stairwell. When Ryan arrived he saw that the horse had managed to get his hind legs stuck in two of the cans.

The horse whinnied and rolled his eyes frantically. At first, Ryan imagined the animal only to be frightened. But even after the horse had calmed down, Ryan realized it was impossible to make him move. For all the weight they carry, a horse's legs are delicate. Perhaps horses realize this themselves for they are terrified of anything that may harm their legs or throw them off balance. A pair of attached rubbish cans seemed ample reason for the horse to stay right where he was.

Crouched headfirst under the stairwell, as if playing some equine game of hide-and-seek, the horse turned and peered woefully at Ryan. Ryan peered back just as woefully. As far as the police officers could see at the moment, the only way to extricate the horse was to tear down the stairs.

Meantime, the landlady kept waving her arms and complaining that New York was no place for law-abiding people.

One of the policemen pushed his cap to the back of his head and put his hands on his hips. "Well," he said, "we'd better get some workmen out here with sledgehammers." He glanced at the stone steps. "It shouldn't take much to knock 'em down."

This did not quiet the landlady in the slightest. "Knock

down the steps, is it?" she cried. "That's all right for the horse—he doesn't have to live here!"

"Wait a minute," Ryan said. He had been studying the horse's position carefully. "You might not have to touch those steps after all." Ryan had decided there was no way in the world to persuade the horse to back out of the stairwell. But he felt pretty sure he could make the horse go forward. However, the only place for the animal to go forward was into the living room.

"You go inside," he told the landlady, "and open your door. I'll lead the horse in—"

"Oh no you won't!" the landlady exploded. "Take a horse into my living room? If you think you're going to . . ."

Ryan tried to explain that she had only two choices: a horse temporarily in her living room or her steps permanently damaged. In any case, she could not leave the horse under the stairs. What, Ryan asked, would the tenants say?

The idea of the tenants seemed to have a profound effect on the landlady. "Well . . ." She hesitated. "All right, you can bring him in. But I warn you: track dirt in my parlor and I'll have the law after you. I don't even let my husband in the living room with his shoes on!"

"Lady," said Ryan, "I promise you. You'll never see a speck of dust."

Leaving the horse under the steps, quite sure the animal wouldn't move until he returned, Ryan went off in search of a ragman. ASPCA calls have taken Ryan into every neighborhood from Park Avenue to Hell's Kitchen; he has learned every nook and cranny, every shop and business. Finding a ragpicker took him no time at all. When he did, Ryan asked for the loan of about fifty burlap bags.

"Buddy," said the ragman, "I collect junk, I collect old clothes and bottles and scrap iron. I buy 'em, I sell 'em—but I don't *lend* 'em!"

"It's for a horse," Ryan said. "I'll bring them right back."

"Oh, for a horse. Sure," said the ragpicker. "That explains everything. You want to make a nice suit for the horse. Look, mister, why don't you go find a custom tailor?"

The ragpicker softened a little after Ryan described the horse's plight. "Okay, okay," the man said. "I got a horse myself. Maybe you help him out someday."

Loaded with burlap bags, Ryan raced back to the house. He spread the bags over the landlady's carpet. With a length of rope, he tied back the chandelier so it wouldn't knock against the horse's head. All Ryan needed was to have the animal bolt through the apartment.

Afraid to look, the landlady opened the door. Very gently, Ryan led the horse, cans and all, into the living room. Inside, the horse appeared gigantic.

The neighbors had gathered to watch the procedure. Unlike their mother, the landlady's children danced with glee.

"Keep it quiet there," Ryan ordered. "The poor fellow's scared enough."

He steadied the horse, lifted one of its hind legs out of the can. He removed the other can just as easily, turned the horse around, led the animal up the steps and into the street. The whole de-canning operation had taken about three minutes.

Ryan untied the chandelier and rolled up the burlap bags. As he had promised, not a speck of dirt had soiled the landlady's rug.

The owner, who eventually recovered his horse, was delighted. The landlady was delighted at getting the animal out of her living room, the policemen were delighted because the business was handled without a riot. The neighbors were gratified, and everyone, in fact, was pleased. Except the landlady's little boy. For a moment, he had believed his parents had finally decided to get him a pony.

2

The Berghs-man

Ryan today is a muscular, jovial wall of a man and he gives the feeling that whatever may be wrong is now going to be all right. Nothing rattles him and probably nothing ever did. At fourteen, single-handed, he conducted a cavalcade of half a dozen horses from Saratoga to New York—a lot of horseflesh to keep under control. This was not the bravado of a wild kid, handsome in the devilish way that only the Irish can be. Ryan had been learning about horses ever since he could walk, and perhaps even before that.

His father, a horse handler in County Limerick, arrived in America as trainer with a string of racing thoroughbreds and stayed on to become a stable manager in and around New York. Born in Manhattan in 1893, Ryan absorbed horse-lore practically by osmosis. Summers, while still in high school, the tall boy with the big grin and more than his share of blarney worked as coachman for one of the wealthy New York families. Later, resplendent in a brass-buttoned scarlet uniform, he put animals through their paces at the American Horse Exchange at 50th and Broadway. Even his father admitted that few boys—or grown men, for that matter—could handle a horse as well as Ryan.

Ryan's boss at the Exchange said much the same, but in a slightly different fashion.

Since Ryan got a commission on every animal sold, he was

naturally eager to show off the horses to their best advantage. Mr. Norris, his boss, had a matched pair of chestnut hackneys, but Norris looked on them more as white elephants than horses. One of the hackneys insisted on running too close to the wooden shaft that kept him in working position. It was a flaw Norris could not correct.

Ryan conceived the simple expedient of switching the horses around. He put the leaner on the outside, where it wouldn't make any difference. By the time Norris realized what Ryan had done, a lady customer came along and bought the hackneys immediately.

After Norris made out the bill of sale and the customer departed, he exploded all over Ryan.

"You crook!" he shouted. "Where did you learn a trick like that? It's the oldest swindle in the game!"

"But all I did—" Ryan began.

"What about the manes?" Norris cried. "You switched the horses, oh, that was clever. Now their manes hang the wrong way!"

This was true. The matched pair had been groomed so that in their original position the manes would hang outward. In Ryan's arrangement, the manes hung inward—an atrocious breach of style.

"Her stableboy can pull the manes," Ryan said defensively. "They'll hang the right way." He gulped and added, "Eventually."

"Oh yes," Norris said sourly, "after he clips them off, weights every hair with lead and combs them out every day for God knows how long. And what kind of a reputation will I have for selling horses like that?"

If Mr. Norris felt so strongly about it, Ryan suggested returning the woman's money.

"Give the money back?" Norris looked at him aghast. "You're a bigger fool than I thought!"

Later, when Norris calmed down, he patted Ryan on the shoulder. "You'll do well," he told the boy. "You have all the instincts of a natural-born horse-gypper."

Ryan smiled. It was the highest compliment a horse-dealer could offer.

After the Exchange, Ryan became a teacher. His pupils were wagon horses at the Lord & Taylor stables, his class-room the streets of Manhattan, his textbooks steamrollers, elevated trains and blowing newspapers. At Lord & Taylor, Ryan was about the only youngster with enough skill to take out a new horse and teach him the facts of city traffic, and not to shy at the more curious human inventions.

His first pupil, the most unmanageable in the stable, bolted as soon as they left the premises. With the wagon lurching crazily, the horse pounding ahead, it seemed to Ryan that he circled Manhattan in the space of five minutes. Ter-rified peddlers abandoned their pushcarts. Pedestrians dashed into the safety of alleyways and shops and wondered why Lord & Taylor was advertising a Wild West show.

At the end, when horse and rider both were winded, Ryan stopped, rubbed down the lathered animal and rubbed down himself. Somehow, during the ride, horse and man had come to know each other and Ryan calmly walked his student back to the stable. As far as the stable manager knew, it had been a quiet jaunt—an impression Ryan did not want cor-rected.

In the course of all this, Ryan developed a certain bounce and resilience and an optimism utterly unquenchable. To-day his grin has not diminished by a centimeter, and the boy still shows in his eyes. But in 1912, he had reason to worry.

Before the end of that year the number of cars in New York nearly doubled, and Ryan knew they were there to stay. His beloved horses were on the way out; nothing could stop it. Ryan met the problem head-on. He taught himself to drive. Alone, as if he had undertaken to master the wildest colt ever foaled, he struggled with the mysteries of the internal-combustion engine—a silent, solitary duel.

By this time, Ryan felt he knew automobiles almost as well as he knew horses—he had taken a car apart piece by piece, bolt by bolt. And put it back together again.

He went to work, then, demonstrating trucks for the Autocar Company. It was, he discovered, not too different from being a pusher on the horse exchange. Instead of horses, he put trucks through their paces. If the prospects liked them, they bought.

Ryan's sales manager had an important deal going. "This outfit's changing over to trucks," he said. "They might order half a dozen of them. But they want somebody to come around and teach their teamsters how to drive."

"Who is it?" Ryan asked.

"Why, it's the dog and cat people," said the manager. "The ASPCA— You know, the Berghs-men."

Ryan, at nineteen, was not too young to have heard the name "Berghs-men" applied to ASPCA workers. It derived from the Society's founder, Henry Bergh, one of the most colorful figures of his day and, on the surface, the least expected to organize such a crusading movement.

Born in 1813, son of a wealthy shipbuilder, the handsome mustachioed Bergh spent almost half his life as a perfect example of the idle rich. His major interests were clothes, dancing, the theater, poetry and music. To pass the time, Bergh and his wife traveled throughout Europe and the Near East. The Berghs knew almost everyone in society, the arts, letters and politics. In 1863, President Lincoln appointed Bergh as Secretary of the American Legation in St. Petersburg.

There, the fifty-year-old man who might have been expected to remain a dandy for the rest of his life changed completely. Once, on the streets of St. Petersburg, the legation secretary noticed a droshky driver beating his horse.

This was such a common sight that it could not even qualify as a picturesque local custom. Yet Bergh made his own driver pull up. Glittering with the gold lace of his office, Bergh commanded the peasant to stop. The Russian obeyed—out of amazement, more than likely, at anyone taking the trouble to notice him.

Every day from then on, Bergh drove through the city discovering similar cases of cruelty and intervening on behalf of the animal.

"At last," Bergh said, "I've found a way to utilize my gold lace—and about the best use that can be made of it."

In an atmosphere where mistreatment of animals, as well as humans, was taken for granted, Bergh's legation colleagues considered his behavior worse than eccentric; it was somehow in bad taste. Above all, they could not understand what had suddenly possessed this former dilettante. Bergh himself never offered an explanation for his changed attitude. Perhaps the idea had been at work unconsciously all these years. During his travels, Bergh had seen enough cruelty to animals to move any sensitive person; he had even noted critical observations in his diary. Whatever the motives, following his Russian experience the prevention of cruelty became the focus of his entire life.

Bergh resigned his legation post. He went to London and conferred with the Earl of Harrowby, president of England's Royal Society for the Prevention of Cruelty to Animals. In 1865, Bergh returned to the United States and began his own work.

Society's degree of civilization, it is said, can be estimated by the status of its women and children. Bergh applied the same yardstick to his country's treatment of animals. Under those terms, New York City qualified as one of the most barbaric in the world. Blood sports were rampant: cockfighting, dogfighting, rat-baiting, bull-baiting. In the everyday business of marketing produce, sheep, calves, cows and pigs were hauled or driven in an agony of broken legs and gouged eyes; chickens were plucked and scalded alive. Even the most basic and valuable transportation animal, the horse, was routinely lashed, beaten with clubs, kicked and goaded. This is not taking into account the pathological tormenting of pets.

Bergh had two points to make. The first was based on an appeal to human decency.

"This is a matter purely of conscience," he said, "it has no perplexing side issues. Politics have no more to do with it than astronomy or the use of globes. No, it is a moral question in all its aspects . . . it is a solemn recognition of that greatest attribute of the Almighty Ruler of the universe, mercy."

Bergh himself, however, realized that the question involved more than mercy. If the average human being is not particularly swayed by moral considerations, he might be expected to respond to self-interest. Bergh's second point was eminently practical.

"Animals contribute in a thousand ways to our comforts and necessities," Bergh said in one of his speeches. He pointed out that nearly 85,000,000 animals worked for the support and profit of his fellow citizens. Every year, cows gave 600,000 pounds of butter, 53,500,000 pounds of cheese, 236,000,000 gallons of milk. Sheep offered 100,000,000 pounds of wool. Market animals were worth $400,000,000 annually; the fisheries, $11,000,000.

"Imagine the consequences if we were to be deprived of all the animals at one time. Could an earthquake or a second deluge be more disastrous? Could we get along without the animals? We could not!"

Bergh made it clear that cruelty, aside from the issue of mercy, would eventually contaminate or destroy some of the country's most valuable natural resources.

In New York, Bergh used all his influence and social contacts to gain backing for his organization. He found one hundred prominent people to endorse the new Society. The group included John T. Hoffman, Mayor of New York, Peter Cooper, John Jacob Astor, William Cullen Bryant, Horace Greeley, Hamilton Fish, Augustus Belmont and James J. Roosevelt.

Immediately afterwards, Bergh left for Albany to receive a state charter of incorporation. Like the American SPCA itself, the charter was the first of its kind in the Western Hemisphere. Bergh also began working for the passage of his anti-cruelty law, to reinforce a statute that had lain dormant in New York State since 1829. Bergh's law proposed that "every person who shall, by his act or neglect, maliciously kill, maim, wound, injure, torture or cruelly beat any horse, mule, cow, cattle, sheep, or other animal belonging to himself or another shall, upon conviction, be adjudged guilty of a misdemeanor." The ASPCA was granted authority to enforce this law.

Bergh set up the first ASPCA headquarters in a couple of attic rooms at Broadway and Fourth Street. Rather than waste money that could further the Society's work, Bergh outfitted the offices with what he called "the very plainest kind of kitchen furniture." The story goes that John Hoffman, who had since become Governor of New York State, while visiting Bergh's headquarters tripped over a hole in the rug.

"Why, Mr. Bergh," said Hoffman, "buy yourself a better carpet and send the bill to me."

"No, thank you, Governor," said Bergh. "But send me the money, and I will put it to better use for the animals."

Bergh's idea of preventing cruelty to animals was plausible, obvious, necessary and, in the long run, beneficial. As a result, and as might have been expected, a great part of the general public opposed it furiously.

Most of the newspapers, relieved to find a pretext for ignoring Boss Tweed and municipal corruption, discovered

Bergh. They launched what may well be the longest, most venomous and vituperative campaign against a single individual in the history of journalism. To begin with, the lean, lanky Bergh, with his top hat, mustache and dandified clothes, made an easy subject for caricature. Operating at first with a staff of three—a young boy, a Negro and a reformed convict —Bergh had to do most of his own legwork. He himself patrolled the streets, issued warnings and even made arrests. Bergh, in effect, was the ASPCA; and the ASPCA was Bergh. Thus, the newspapers had a neat, compact target.

From the beginning, Bergh suffered constant journalistic abuse. When he managed to win some improvement in the treatment of livestock, the *Herald* wrote mockingly:

> Calves now ride to market in a sort of triumph, sitting upright with that calm, unsophisticated expression peculiar to Horace Greeley and other persons from the country.

The *Sunday Mercury* added:

> The mild and gentle countenance of the poor calves, and the rush of blood to the head which disturbs the reflections of doomed capons, touches the heart of the gentle Bergh. . . . The Egyptians worshipped crocodiles and bull-calves, and we this day maintain a set of high priests of the same denomination.

Once, Bergh protested the treatment of sea turtles shipped into New York harbor. It was current practice to store the living creatures on their backs, with ropes run through holes gouged in their fins. Bergh went so far as to arrest one schooner captain and his crew. Bergh lost his case when the court, through an interpretation which only the legal mind can explain, decided that the law was made for animals and turtles were not animals.

With the turtle case, Bergh became fair game for anyone feeling the need to demonstrate his wit. The *Herald* devoted six columns to the trial. One restaurant owner displayed a turtle with its head resting on a pillow. Bergh was called "a maudlin sympathizer with persecuted rats and unfortunate bedbugs." The ASPCA began to receive calls that a horse, unblanketed, was being left to stand all night in a snowstorm. Bergh investigated. The horse was made of wood. Someone else complained that a butcher had hung a raccoon by the tail from an iron bar. It was true. The raccoon had been hanging there for a month—stuffed.

Bergh had his own public supporters in the matter: Louis Agassiz, the great naturalist; Horace Greeley; and, later, Harriet Beecher Stowe and her brother, Henry Ward Beecher.

The truth of the matter was that Bergh welcomed attack as much as he welcomed encouragement. Anything, he knew, was better than being ignored.

He called the *Herald*'s satire "the greatest service I have ever had. . . . And to the funny fellow who wrote that account, I have always felt grateful, for his ridicule awakened the public from its apathy. Next day, one million people understood my purpose, and, in a week, more millions knew that there was a Society for the defense of inferior animals."

Within two years, other states and cities adopted Bergh's reforms: Buffalo, Philadelphia, Boston, San Francisco. By 1869, there were SPCA's in Maine, New Jersey, Texas, Massachusetts and Canada.

In New York, the ASPCA managed to scrape together enough money to keep functioning: from a few charitable contributions by the public, a couple of modest bequests, and, as always, from Bergh's own resources which he continued to pour into the organization.

To many of the newspapers and a segment of the public, Bergh remained a target of ridicule. Even his staff workers were not exempt, and the abuse was not always verbal. Watching a parade, one Berghs-man saw the driver of a butcher's wagon bring his horse to a stop by gashing its nose with an iron barb on a stick. When the Berghs-man tried to prevent this, the spectators knocked him down and nearly beat him to death. (The newspapers called Bergh and his men "overzealous.")

When Bergh finally succeeded in preventing the over-loading of horsecars, the operating companies screamed that he was trying to ruin them. When he protested the use of painful checkreins, agonizing burr-bits and the docking of horses' tails, the horse lovers of New York rose up against him in righteous indignation. When he inspected slaughter-houses, butchers threw viscera in his face.

Bergh did not confine his work to preventing cruelty to animals. In 1874, a woman implored Bergh to help a ten-year-old girl who had been repeatedly whipped and muti-lated by her foster mother. The charitable societies had no legal basis for action; statutes against cruelty to children did not exist. Bergh acted in the only way open to him. He had the child, little Mary Ellen, brought to court on the grounds that humans were animals—and as animals deserved the protection of the law.

Jacob Riis was in court when Bergh and his lawyer associ-ate, Elbridge Gerry, presented the case.

"I saw a child brought in," Riis wrote, "carried in a horse blanket, at the sight of which men wept aloud. I saw it laid at the feet of the judge, who turned his face away, and in the stillness of that courtroom I heard the voice of Henry Bergh. 'The child is an animal,' he said. 'If there is no justice for it as a human being, it shall at least have the rights of the cur in the street. It shall not be abused.' And as I looked I knew I was where the first chapter of the children's rights was writ-ten, under warrant of that made for the dog."

The court sent Mary Ellen to a home for children; the

foster mother received a one-year jail sentence. But Bergh
had realized that a society for the prevention of cruelty to
animals was not enough.

Bergh founded the Society for the Prevention of Cruelty
to Children in 1875—with much the same journalistic reaction that had greeted the ASPCA. Bergh had always been
criticized for worrying more about animals than humans.
Now that he planned to give some attention to humans, at
least of the younger ages, the *World* offered this comment
on Bergh's proposed legislation:

> It is announced that Mr. Bergh's preposterous bill for
> clothing him with the power to discipline all the naughty
> children of New York is to be the special order of the day in
> Albany. We sincerely hope that it may not finally be kicked
> out of the Legislature, as it richly deserves to be, until the
> public mind shall have had time to get itself thoroughly
> enlightened as to the state of things in which it has become
> possible for such a person as Henry Bergh to bring the Legisla-
> ture to the point of seriously entertaining such an impudently
> senseless measure.

The Legislature, surprisingly, passed this "impudently
senseless measure." John D. Wright became the SPCC's first
president. Bergh served as vice-president, with Peter Cooper,
Theodore Roosevelt, Cornelius Vanderbilt and others, and
continued to put most of his effort into the ASPCA.

The biggest surprise about the ASPCA was not the public's initial rejection. More amazing, in spite of everything,
the Society got things done. At first, the ASPCA progressed
by inches. Twenty years may be the saturation point in over-
coming resistance to a valuable idea. This, at least, was how
long it took the Society. After two decades of constant ex-
posure to the ASPCA's work, the public finally began to think
that this man Bergh might have something after all. The
ASPCA had established animal (and human) drinking fountains, prevented disease by its insistence on sanitary butcher-

ing, saved the meat industry millions by suggesting improved transportation methods; it had relieved the sufferings of thousands of work animals and pets. By the late 1880's, New Yorkers had taken the Society pretty much for granted; it was an accepted institution and they would have been furious had anyone suggested curtailing its activities.

Bergh himself had little time to enjoy the public's change of heart. He died on March 12, during the blizzard of 1888. P. T. Barnum, who had tangled with Bergh many times, went to the graveside. The enormous wreath he left was worthy of the greatest showman on earth. His remarks were less flamboyant and more deeply felt: "Henry Bergh is to be honored and respected for his unselfish devotion to such an excellent cause."

Fifteen years before, Henry Ward Beecher had written a whimsical article envisioning Bergh's funeral. "Will there not be a commotion among animals?" the preacher asked. "Without a doubt," he continued, "all good men will attend. The birds will tell it. The beasts of the field will know it. Even tropical turtles will feel briny tears."

Imagining Bergh's entry into Heaven, Beecher went on: "Airy elephants will bear him up; the spirit of released horses will prance upon him; and Maltese grimalkins will purr celestial satisfaction, and rub his legs with their most beseeching caresses. Dogs without number, woolly, hairy or silk-coated, will turn their lustrous eyes upon him with refulgent gratitude. Yes, the whole air will be full of emancipated animals, pressing around like those backgrounds of heads in the pictures of the old masters, all tenderly eager to greet and honor the benefactor of animals."

Perhaps, in 1888, it had been just that way.

The Society Bergh founded was the "dog and cat people" interested in buying motor ambulances from Ryan's boss. By virtue of its founding date, it was the oldest humane society in the Western Hemisphere, and, as an organization, rapidly becoming the most extensive. Since 1894, New York had put the Society in charge of dog-licensing for New York City. The ASPCA operated a shelter for stray animals. It had a whole staff of special agents to investigate complaints of cruelty, to check conditions in stockyards and slaughterhouses, markets, livestock auctions. In its rescue work, the Society was the best friend a horse—or dog or cat—could have in New York. That summer of 1912, the Society had just opened a full-scale animal hospital. Two years before, a patroness had donated two motor ambulances, but the Society's work had so increased that now it needed more vehicles.

"This might turn into a good account," said the sales manager. "I want you to go over there and really show them what these trucks can do."

Ryan promised to do his best, although in a way he felt he was sabotaging some of his best friends. As soon as a driver had been retrained to handle a truck, his team was put out to pasture on a nearby farm. Thus, the harder Ryan worked, the more horses would be retired.

Few of the drivers had ever handled a truck before. To some, Ryan had to explain the operations in terms of "Giddap!" and "Whoa!" There were times, at the end of a hard day, when Ryan himself mixed horsemanship with truckmanship. "Rein her up," he would shout when he wanted a student to apply the brakes.

The training course finally ended. Only one horse-drawn vehicle remained: the Society's enormous red and gold horse ambulance with brass mountings and patent leather upholstery. The famous ambulance had all the style and dash of a fire engine, the brilliance of a circus wagon and, to Ryan, it was the most glamorous, gorgeous vehicle in the world.

One of the ASPCA officials noticed him admiring it one day. "Quite a rig, isn't it?" he said.

Ryan agreed. "When do you replace it?" he asked.

"Oh, I don't think we'll change this one for quite a while," the Berghs-man said. "Why?"

"I just wondered," Ryan answered.

Next day, before he was due to return to the automotive firm, Ryan stopped for a last look at the red and gold ambulance. The ASPCA man met him again.

"Say," he said, "I hear you're a good man with trucks."

"I know how to drive them," Ryan said.

"I hear you're pretty good with horses, too," the man went on.

"I've been driving horses longer than I've been driving trucks," Ryan admitted.

"You're pretty good with animals in general, aren't you," the Berghs-man added. "Why don't you work with us? We need men like you."

Ryan hesitated a moment.

"You can start with that ambulance," the Berghs-man went on quickly.

Ryan blinked. "*That* ambulance? With a horse, not a motor?"

"That's right."

"You know what?" Ryan said. "You just hired me."

Ryan's career as a truck demonstrator ended that day. It was an opportunity to work with his beloved horses again, and the sight of the red and gold ambulance might have tipped the balance. Ryan, indeed, was always to be involved to one degree or another with horses. What he did not know, at the time, was that he would also be involved with practically every animal that came out of the Ark.

3

The Monkey House

The first animal off the Ark must have been a monkey. If monkeys then were anything like they are now, he came bursting out full of beans and looking for mischief. His descendants have been doing so ever since. Compared to human beings, they show every sign of being smarter, quicker and more fiendish. Ryan is one man who appreciates this. Although originally devoted to horses, Ryan learned about monkeys in a hurry (with monkeys, this is the best way to do it).

They are, Ryan discovered, much like children. But very old children, very precocious children, with prehensile tails as added equipment. On the one hand, monkeys crave affection; they can be wistful, pleading, and downright angelic when they have a mind to do so. On the other hand, they can show all the refined and subtle sense of humor of a four-year-old practical joker. They also enjoy the feeling of being one up on you. They are often jittery, excitable, boisterous; they lose their tempers, throw tantrums, sulk and give the impression of brooding on the wicked ways of the world.

With this personality, monkeys have naturally found a compatible atmosphere in Manhattan. No one (except perhaps the ASPCA) can say for sure how many monkeys have run loose in New York—or may be running loose at this moment. This is hardly surprising, for there is little demand for that type of census data. The more startling thought is that any monkeys at all are running loose. Yet not long ago Ryan captured four of them in the vicinity of the American Telephone and Telegraph Building in downtown New York.

One by one, he lured them into boxes baited with fruit, carted them back to the shelter and eventually transferred them to the zoo. He never did discover where they came from, how they reached the AT&T Building, or what they wanted at the offices of this great utility. AT&T shares have always made an excellent investment, but even Ryan does not credit monkeys with this kind of foresight.

On another occasion, Ryan had a telephone call from a policeman at a boardinghouse. The monkey, whose owner had died and left the animal to fend for himself, was still living in the room. He showed no inclination to move out, and the landlady had found prospective tenants reluctant to share quarters with him. She had tried everything to persuade the monkey to vacate. He only jabbered at her and made what she believed to be insulting gestures. Finally, as if he had been any ordinary lodger behind in his rent, she called the police.

One officer had been dispatched to the boardinghouse. He decided he needed reinforcements. The reinforcements decided they needed Ryan.

"What's all the fuss over a monkey?" Ryan asked. He could hear excited voices in the background.

"We can't get hold of him," the policeman said. "There's a cage here, but he won't go in it."

"You boys disappoint me," Ryan said. "Just put on a pair of gloves, pick him up gently and put him in the cage."

"Yeah?" said the policeman. "This monkey's as big as an airedale. You try it."

"All right," said Ryan cheerfully, "so I will."

Ryan packed his monkey equipment into an ASPCA truck: a pole with a lasso on the end for catching the monkey, and a screen-sided box to hold the monkey after Ryan caught him.

When he reached the boardinghouse, Ryan saw that the policeman had not been accurate. The monkey was not a monkey, but a red ape. He was not the size of an airedale; he was much bigger. He was also in a foul temper. He squawked, huffed, grunted, bared his teeth, and Ryan could easily understand why the landlady had considered herself insulted.

"Well," Ryan mused, "he is a big one, isn't he?"

"Just put on a pair of gloves," one of the officers advised, "and put him in the cage."

The ape, meanwhile, bounced up and down on the bed, clambered over the furniture and finally perched on the top of his own cage. There he sat, shaking his shoulders and muttering irritably. He took hold of the cage bars and rattled them loudly, curled up his lips and made disagreeable noises at Ryan.

"You stop that," Ryan ordered. He pointed at the cage door. "You just get in there and behave yourself."

The ape gave Ryan a look of surprise, hesitated a moment, then obediently climbed down and entered the cage. He even closed the door behind him.

"I'll be damned," said one policeman.

"You have to know how to talk to them," Ryan said modestly.

The officers were still shaking their heads in admiration when Ryan went downstairs again to get the truck ready. On his way back to the room, Ryan noticed a red ape walking determinedly down the banister. He looked like a man on his way to an important business deal.

Ryan did a classic double take. Before he could move, the ape padded into the vestibule, opened the door and disappeared into the street. Ryan had left his lasso and box upstairs. He raced to the room.

"Why didn't you tell me there were two of them?" he said.

"There aren't," said an officer. "There's only one. As soon as you went out, he reached through the bars and opened the door."

"Why didn't you stop him?" Ryan said with exasperation.

"We don't know how to talk to him," the policeman answered. "You see, we do most of our work with felons. It's not the same. . . ."

Ryan grabbed his equipment and ran down to the street again. He saw no sign of the ape. A moment later, he heard a stream of chattering. The ape had climbed a girder of the elevated train structure. He perched there and beat his chest.

"Get down!" Ryan called. "You go back in that cage." This time, Ryan's persuasiveness did not work. The ape hid behind a girder. A small crowd had already gathered and was watching Ryan with interest. Even in New York it was not usual to see a solid-looking, uniformed officer yelling into the empty air.

The ape reappeared on another girder. "Hey, mister," an onlooker said, tugging Ryan's sleeve, "didja see the monk up there?"

"Oh, shut up," Ryan muttered.

The policemen came out and tried to keep the crowd from blocking traffic. Seeing the audience below, the ape revealed a new aspect of his personality. Snuffling gleefully, he waved at the spectators, put his hands above his head and wiggled his fingers. The ape, Ryan decided, should have been in show business.

Like a human hoofer, the ape paraded back and forth along the girders, clapping his hands or raising them in the manner of a victorious prizefighter. He struck poses and even seemed to wait for applause.

"All he needs is a cane and a straw hat," one of the officers remarked. "I've seen worse in vaudeville."

The ape jumped to the roof of a passing streetcar. Ryan

yelled at the conductor who, apparently thinking Ryan was only a passenger waiting to board, instinctively speeded up. With a long arm held aloft, in the posture of the Statue of Liberty, the ape stood on the roof. In despair, Ryan imagined the streetcar bearing the animal far away, into the depths of Queens.

The ape sprang off just in time. He reached the top of a parked car in one bound. In another, he leaped to the front of the boardinghouse and climbed up the brownstone façade. At a second-floor window sill he stopped, turned around and gave a triumphant chuckle.

"Say, he's pretty good," a policeman observed. "He doesn't need the ASPCA. What he wants is a booking agent."

The ape was out of range of Ryan's lasso. Ryan began figuring ways of luring him down. He turned to one of the policemen.

"Got any fruit?" he asked.

"Only a ham sandwich in my lunch box," the officer said. "But I know a fruit stand around the corner."

"I need a couple of bananas," Ryan said.

"Sure." The officer left and returned a few moments later. In one hand he held a bunch of bananas; in the other, an apple which he munched on.

Ryan peeled the banana halfway down and waved it in the air. The ape looked at it with mild interest. Ryan tossed the fruit into the box. He had already rigged the lid with a cord, so that he could pull it shut as soon as the ape entered.

The ape did not enter. Ryan peeled another banana and ate part of it.

"Yum, yum, yum," Ryan called. "Boy, this is sure a good banana." The ape did not seem convinced.

Ryan tried again, with even more enthusiastic expressions, smacking his lips, patting his stomach and shouting *"Yum! Yum!"* at the top of his voice. He consumed the best part of three. The police squad also joined in the banana eating.

Very gingerly, the ape climbed down from his perch and sidled up to the box.

"Quiet now," Ryan ordered.

The ape peered and sniffed. Finally, he jumped inside. He picked up a half-eaten banana but tossed it down again. Something else had caught his eye.

Ryan pulled the cord and the lid dropped into place. The ape paid no attention. He looked perfectly content in the box.

"Geez," said a policeman, "I thought you were going to lose him again."

"No," Ryan said. "I knew if I could get him inside he'd stay there a while."

"He didn't want the bananas after all," said the officer.

"He'll eat them later," Ryan said. "Right now, he's busy." He pointed to the far wall of the box, where the ape sat happily making faces at himself in a mirror.

"Never go after a monkey without a mirror," Ryan said. "Did you ever see anybody pass a mirror without stopping to look in it? Monkeys are the same way. Especially this one. After I saw him clowning around up there, I figured he couldn't resist it. The banana was just to get him to realize there was a mirror in the box."

Ryan hoisted the box into the truck, then mopped his forehead with a handkerchief. "Well," he said, heaving a sigh of relief. "I hope I don't have to do that again for a while."

"Tough work," the policeman sympathized.

"No, not so much that," Ryan said. "It's the damned bananas. I'm allergic to them!"

Most of the monkeys Ryan has met do not normally frequent boardinghouses or office buildings. They prefer, instead, the waterfront and docksides. A lot of them escape from ships putting into New York from tropical ports. Like sailors and stevedores, stray monkeys hang around the piers, the customs sheds and the warehouses. Possibly they enjoy the exotic, international flavor; or they may be waiting for transportation back home.

One monkey, a little capuchin who had acquired the name "Sally," lived on the waterfront for five months. She cadged food from the dockhands or swiped it from cargo vessels and lunch wagons. No one knew Sally's address, for she always dashed away to a nest she had arranged for herself, hidden somewhere in the maze of alleyways and old buildings.

With winter coming on, the stevedores began worrying about Sally. They called Ryan to see if he could catch her. Sally herself must have been concerned about the weather. Ryan lured her into a cage with nothing more complicated than a glass of milk. But he took no credit for it.

"She wanted to be caught," he admitted.

Sally was such a gentle, friendly animal that Ryan himself adopted her. Once in his apartment, however, the situation changed. Sally turned partial to Mrs. Ryan. Whenever Ryan came near, Sally would leap into Mrs. Ryan's arms and scream invective at the baffled humane officer.

"Sometimes I think she's a gold-digger at heart," Ryan said. "She got what she wanted, and after that . . . Oh well," he shrugged. "I'm not the first."

Eventually Ryan gave Sally to another agent at the shelter. "You take her," he said. "It's not that I don't like her. But it's embarrassing. When anybody from the Society stops in for a visit, she acts like I've been beating her. I mean, it just doesn't look right."

Sally, with her five months on the waterfront, might have established some kind of record for loose monkeys in New York. The Professor, another capuchin, was at liberty only five weeks. He more than made up for this brief period by sheer brilliance, audacity, dazzling footwork, strategy and tactics that very nearly disrupted all of the North River shipping.

As far as Ryan could reconstruct the case, the Professor escaped from a freighter that had tied up at Pier 62. Ryan could not be sure whether the Professor had belonged to a sailor or whether the monkey had been a stowaway. As he came to know the Professor better, Ryan decided he must have been a stowaway; and he often wondered why, during the course of the voyage, the Professor had not bothered to take over the whole ship.

In any case, the Professor arrived in New York with all the enthusiasm and dedication of a man convinced that his fortune lay within his grasp. The first indication was not slow in coming.

A couple of longshoremen were having a snack at a waterfront lunch counter when something brown flashed in and out again.

"My God, Charlie, what was that?" asked one of them.

"I don't know," said the second, his coffee cup still poised at his lips. "A cat, probably. Funny. I could have sworn it looked like a monkey."

During the days that followed, the lunch counter customers realized very clearly that it was a monkey. The Professor, like any competent guerilla general, had scouted out a supply base. From then on, he raided it consistently and thoroughly.

The Professor would burst in unexpectedly and, in the ensuing confusion, load his arms with bags of potato chips and be on his way before the proprietor or customers could recover their wits. He swiped sandwiches from the plates and, chattering triumphantly, dashed off with his loot. If the customers chased him outside, the Professor would shinny up a pole and pelt them with leftovers. Once, the Professor even stole a coffee cup.

"What, for God's sake, does he want with a coffee cup?"

the startled customer asked. (The Professor had not taken the contents, which now soaked the customer's lap.)

"Beats me," said the proprietor, helping to mop up. "Maybe he gets his coffee someplace else."

The lunch counterman complained to the pier captain. The Professor was wrecking his business. The captain promised action. The situation had become more urgent. In addition to the lunch counter, the Professor had extended his theater of operations to a five-block area. Moving from one warehouse to the next, the Professor broke open cases of figs, nuts and kippered herring.

Classifying the Professor as a deportable alien or as contraband merchandise, the customs guards set after him. The Professor conducted a successful rearguard action by throwing kippers at them.

The pier captain mobilized flying squads of longshoremen. They had no better luck. The Professor had his headquarters deep among the rafters and girders of the pier. Even the longshoremen could not follow his trail. Within a month, the Professor had broken up about five hundred dollars' worth of goods and the port area had fallen into a state of total confusion.

At that point, the captain called for Ryan. "Listen," he said, "this monkey is a genius. A criminal genius, but a genius. Take my word for it."

"Go on," Ryan said. "I never saw one I couldn't handle."

He would remember that remark in the week to come.

Because the captain had been so forceful in detailing the Professor's ability, Ryan decided to bring along his friend Bob Coles, another of the Society's agents. The monkey, Ryan thought, might be smarter than either of them individually, but certainly not together. Ryan had time to wonder about that, too.

Ryan and Coles began with standard procedure: a baited box and a mirror. For a while, Ryan set up as many mirrors as a millinery department. But the Professor had no interest in self-admiration; nor did he show any enthusiasm for food. The first day, Ryan had used bananas and other fruits. The Professor scorned them.

"Okay," Ryan said. "And he doesn't like vegetables. So maybe he likes meat."

Next day, Ryan tried a different lure: a pork chop. The Professor wouldn't even sniff at it. Ryan and Coles, defeated, ended up eating the pork chop for lunch.

Ryan thought a lot about the Professor throughout the following week. He began to see the monkey as a cross between Albert Einstein and Lucky Luciano.

"He's clever," Ryan admitted. "Maybe that's where we're making our mistake. The ordinary stuff doesn't work with him. We've got to be as clever as he is. We've got to use our imaginations."

The next device was indeed an imaginative one. Ryan had invented it just for the occasion. The idea had come to him at about three in the morning, while he had been tossing restlessly and pondering over the Professor. It was a loaded coconut.

Ryan drilled a one-inch hole in the coconut, emptied out the milk and packed it with chopped bananas. "Here's the way I see it," Ryan told Coles. "If the Professor reaches in and grabs the banana, he won't be able to get his hand out again."

"Why not?" Coles asked. "All he needs to do is let go."

"I don't think he will," Ryan said. "When he has a fistful of banana, I don't think he'll realize that he has to drop it if he wants to get loose."

"Suppose you're right?" Coles said. "What do you end up with? A monkey with a coconut on his hand."

"No, you don't see the point," Ryan said. "The coconut's bound to get jammed in a beam or crossbar. Then he'll be stuck. We can climb up and bring him down."

Ryan put his plan into effect. The two men watched breathlessly while the Professor plunged his hand into the coconut. As Ryan had predicted, the Professor's fist was too full of banana to slip back through the hole. Ryan did not foresee what happened next.

The Professor merely swung his arm in a great arc and shattered the coconut against a girder.

Ryan and Coles went back to the shelter. Neither said anything for a while.

"We have brains," Ryan said at last. "We can think things through. That's one advantage we have on the Professor. We can analyze. We can figure things out."

"I'm not so damned sure of that any more," said Coles. "Not with the Professor."

"Our whole approach is wrong," Ryan said. "We've been trying to get to him with things he basically doesn't want. The Professor doesn't care about food. He's got warehouses loaded with it."

"What we have to figure," Ryan went on, "is this: what's the one thing he wants that he doesn't have now?"

Coles' face lit up. "You mean . . . ?"

"That's right," Ryan said. "Tomorrow we call the zoo and we borrow a girl monkey."

The zoo does not usually loan out simian Mata Haris, but the curator agreed to allow Ryan the services of a female capuchin named Mike. At the waterfront, Ryan set up a block-and-tackle to operate the sliding door of the cage. In the back wall of the cage, he drilled a hole and ran a long line through it. At one end of the line was Mike; at the other, Ryan. Coles stood by to operate the block-and-tackle.

·Mike's chirping attracted the Professor almost immediately. He climbed down from a crossbeam and strutted back and forth, trying to impress the new arrival. Each time the Professor came near Mike, Ryan drew up a little on the leash and brought her closer to the cage.

Mike was a perfect Lorelei. She shrugged her shoulders, pranced up and down, giggling and tittering. Ryan had no idea what she might be telling the Professor, but it sounded inviting. And for the Professor himself, it was love at first sight. From the terror of the waterfront and snatcher of kippers, the Professor had changed to an ardent Romeo.

The two monkeys came closer to the cage. Jabbering and ogling Mike, the Professor reached out for her. With seductive indignation, Mike scuttled into the cage. The Professor, leering happily as if he had finally persuaded Mike to see his etchings, leaped after her. Coles lowered the door.

"Well," Ryan said. "Let that be a lesson for you."

"Too late," Coles said. "I'm already married."

The Professor and Mike were getting along famously when Ryan and Coles drove them both to a calm domestic future at the zoo.

"He knows he's been caught," Ryan said, "but I don't think he cares."

4

The Society

Monkeys, of course, aren't the only animals rating the Society's attention. In New York, today, cats (or kangaroos) can do a lot better than sitting around looking at kings. From the Society, a cat or a kangaroo—or any other animal—can get royal treatment in the way of medical care, food, shelter, service and equipment. Affection is available in king-size quantities, too, although not measurable statistically.

The Society cares for upwards of 270,000 animals a year and spends close to $2,000,000 doing it—a budget including such items as 48 tons of dog food, 5 tons of cat food and 25 tons of yesterday's newspapers. The ASPCA operates nine shelters, one of them recently rebuilt in the Bronx at a cost well above $250,000. Within the past five years, the Society has constructed the $350,000 Animalport for animal air travelers at Idlewild terminal; added a $60,000 pathology section to its new $1,000,000 hospital-shelter-headquarters at 92nd Street and York Avenue in Manhattan. Veterinary staff has increased from 9 to 14. The Society is still in the midst of the most profound reorganization and expansion program in its history.

Before this reorganization, the ASPCA risked falling into the predicament of the man who arrived at one of the shelters and asked the Society to take charge of a 600-pound Galápagos tortoise he had at home. It was a little too much for him, the man admitted, and he really didn't think he could give the tortoise proper care.

The Society, perpetually confronted with personnel problems involving stray whales, grizzly bears and other creatures, found a berth for the tortoise at the New York Aquarium. But, like the tortoise-owner, the Society feared it would soon be overwhelmed by the size of its own task and the limitations of its own resources. For instance—the Supervisor of Humane Work, then only a department even though representing the Society's very reason for existence, didn't even have a secretary, typed most of his own letters, coped with constantly ringing phones, tried to cover a greater New York metropolitan area with only seven uniformed agents, and got otherwise bogged down in clerical impedimenta.

William Rockefeller, ASPCA President since 1956 and one of the youngest men ever to hold that office, had a young man's answer. Rockefeller, Yale '40 and a partner in a prominent Manhattan law firm, made it clear that he didn't give a rap how the Society had operated before but how it was going to operate now and in the future.

No figurehead, the Society's President works as hard as anybody else, sparking ideas and providing leadership to see them through (at a salary of zero per year, the same non-wage rate as that for the ASPCA Board of Managers).

The idea Rockefeller sparked was this: the Society, a non-profit organization, should function as efficiently and smoothly as any modern corporation—and even more efficiently, to make best use of limited funds. Struggling along with outmoded management methods was false economy. Straitjacketed by insufficient staff and working tools, the Society might end up doing an insufficient job.

Rockefeller called in a well-known firm of management consultants who analyzed every aspect of the Society's operations. (Humane Work, the firm suggested, should be a full-fledged division of the Society with a director, not a supervisor, and with enough special agents and clerical help to do a creditable job. This was only one of several hundred recommendations.) In this case, efficiency didn't mean cutting back. It meant expansion: more staff, more equipment, more office space. With Rockefeller's inspiration, the society not only began to enjoy its face-lifting but started thinking of even bolder projects.

Talking about the newly built $60,000 pathology lab, William Mapel, ASPCA Administrative Vice-President, says:

"We'd like the same kind of expansion program in every one of our departments. There's no end to this thing, and once the idea gets around that improvements have to be made there is no dearth of dollar-spending suggestions. Thus it is that a lot of ideas get thrown out. For those adopted we scratch and scratch for money."

Missouri-born, Mapel is a tall, good-looking man with a silvery mustache and a soft spot for Irish setters. A graduate of the University of Missouri, a college professor, Director of Washington and Lee's School of Journalism, holder of a traveling fellowship to Europe, Mapel has also been a much-honored newspaper executive. In 1958 he retired as President of the Publishers' Association of New York City after 17 years that "almost did the old boy in." With a career that would normally have taken at least two men to achieve, Mapel enjoys being slightly on the shady side of sixty. "One of the delights of being old," he grins, "is that you don't have to pretend you know all the answers." The truth is that Mapel, like everyone else in the Society, thinks young and acts young. The youthful outlook, combined with repeated applications of hard work, is one of the things moving the Society into renaissance.

While nothing in the Society's history equals the rejuvenation going on today, the ASPCA has in fact shown constant growth ever since its founding in 1866. Colonel Alfred Wagstaff, first Society President to begin an administration in the twentieth century, led in establishing the most complete hospital for animals the humane movement had ever seen, and a Brooklyn shelter then called the most modern in existence.

During Wagstaff's 1906-1921 administration, longest of any Society President, the emphasis shifted from horses to smaller animals, although, as late as 1918, the Society still needed 25 men to operate the Society's horse-watering service. During World War I, Wagstaff protested sending tens of thousands of horses and mules abroad; it was ridiculous enough for people to be shooting at each other, let alone animals. With other humane organizations, the Society joined in forming the American Red Star Animal Relief to furnish medical supplies, instruments, bandages and horse ambulances to the Veterinary Corps.

With New York having become the country's pre-Hollywood movie capital, the Society had problems restraining the wilder flights of cinematic fancy. Following the Society's complaint, a judge convicted one movie director of forcing a horse, in the interest of reality, to jump off a 43-foot cliff.

While protecting movie animals came as a new and unexpected wrinkle, the Society still had to cope with old familiar troubles. As they seem destined to do forever, cats and dogs fell out of windows, swallowed stones, bones and hatpins. Between 1912 and 1916, the hospital had cared for 25,000 patients. By the early 20's, the average annual admission figures had practically doubled. More hospital cases needed surgery, and Society veterinarians pioneered work in animal anesthesia. Today, the new pathology lab continues its cancer research, but as early as 1920 it had already begun a cooperative program with Memorial Hospital, using radium treatments.

"The city is running away with us!" cried Frank K. Sturgis, Society President from 1921 to 1932.

Society agents of that era patrolled a metropolis of

6,000,000 people, covering 309 square miles and about 4,496 miles of streets; the Society's 47 ambulances covered 880,000 miles in one 18-month period—about 2,000 miles a day.

Under Sturgis, the Society began its own building boom, adding to the Brooklyn Shelter, constructing new shelters in the Bronx, Staten Island and Queens. For the third time since 1912, the Society expanded its hospital, putting up a four-story addition that tripled the hospital's capacity. The April 1925 issue of *Veterinary Medicine* remarked:

> The equipment of this institution is little short of marvelous . . . it is a pity there is not a veterinary college in New York City so beautifully planned and equipped. As one of our visitors stated, he has been in practically every institution in Europe and has never seen anything comparable to this place.

On top of running the hospital, Chief Veterinarian Dr. Raymond J. Garbutt acquired another duty: giving weekly talks on animal care over a brand-new communications medium, radio.

The Society, in 1928, sheltered its first two lions—one a lioness who added to this population by presenting the Society with three cubs born in the hospital. During that same period other patients, among the 10,000, included a camel that had caught pneumonia while starring in a Passion Play, and a cat who had somehow contrived to get himself ignominiously and thoroughly stuck on flypaper.

Presidents George M. Woolsey (1932-1937) and Alexander S. Webb (1937-1948) had the intricate task of steering the Society through the Depression, when as much as 70 percent of hospital admissions were charity ones. Pet owners who could ill afford a doctor for themselves crowded the waiting rooms with ailing animals. One day, the place was so jammed that Alexander Webb could hardly make his way to the offices. "Hey, you!" a dog-owner shouted at the elegant, impeccably dressed President. "You wait your turn!"

Society workers took voluntary salary cuts rather than cur-
tail any ASPCA services. Even at that, the flood of new patients strained facilities so much that Dr. Garbutt pleaded:
"Those who are about to acquire pets should realize that unless they have the means of caring for them properly . . .
they would be far wiser not to assume the responsibility of
ownership." Needless to say, pet owners did not follow Garbutt's advice. Between 1930 and 1937, the first year of
Webb's administration, hospital cases doubled. Minor details
such as possible bankruptcy have never much influenced animal lovers.

After the Society weathered the Depression, World War
II added bizarre problems of its own. In addition to giving
courses in animal aid in case of bombings, and working out
a detailed program of emergency care, the Society had to
figure out what to do about dog licenses. In a metal shortage,
the Society ordered licenses made of pressed fiber. They
must have been tasty, for a lot of dogs promptly chewed
them up. The Government banned production of ready-
made dog or cat food, and the Society had to contrive a new
animal diet including chicken heads and feet, fish heads,
vegetables and table scraps. With canned milk severely ra-
tioned, the Society's purchasing agent knocked himself out
locating powdered milk for cats. He finally found 200 pounds
in Wisconsin, and had it rushed to New York. The cats
wouldn't even taste the stuff.

Just before the end of the war, an outbreak of rabies over-
burdened the Society's facilities and finances. The Board of
Health ruled that any dog even remotely suspected of being
in contact with a rabid animal had to be quarantined six
months in an ASPCA shelter. The Society soon found itself
up to its ears in dogs and swamped with new expenses—to
say nothing of protests from furious owners. In 1944, the
Society protested the unnecessary strictness of the quaran-

tine and asked for modifications. In a huff, Mayor Fiorello La Guardia not only refused but threatened to deprive the ASPCA of dog license money it had been collecting since 1894. But New Yorkers assailed the Legislature with so many blistering letters that the Little Flower's bill withered and died in committee.

In 1948, a crisis nearly forced the Society to close its doors. The Veterans Administration decided to build a hospital at Avenue A and 24th Street, site of the ASPCA's own hospital, garage and Manhattan Shelter since 1912. The Federal Government awarded $304,000 for the condemned property, barely enough to buy a vacant lot in Manhattan. Duplicating the building would cost nearly three times that amount. With its new President, John T. Beals, Jr., the Society appealed the decision and meanwhile launched a fund-raising campaign to fill a $500,000 gap.

Construction began and, after two years of delays and setbacks, Society trucks moved material and equipment into the still unfinished building. Cargo included 100 dogs, half a dozen cats—and one squirrel.

The courts eventually increased the award to cover about half the new construction costs. Despite the financial hardship, one good thing emerged: the Society gained a sparkling new million-dollar shelter and hospital, a showpiece in the humane movement.

Another storm broke in 1949. Following the hassle with La Guardia, the Society continued to collect dog license fees. Originally, the Legislature had intended this revenue to reimburse the Society for operating its animal shelters. A lot had happened since 1894. Shelter service had increased. The license fee hadn't. The difference between the money coming in and the cost of shelter service amounted to a stunning deficit. President Beals led the Society in asking the Legislature to increase the fee—for the first time in 55 years. Licenses had been $2, renewals, $1; and the Legislature finally agreed to raise new licenses and renewals to $3. A drop in the bucket; but the Society, by this time, had learned to live on drops in the bucket.

The Society also had to learn to live with controversy. In 1952, some of the most kindhearted people in the world stood up at one of the Society's Annual Meetings and shouted insults at ASPCA executives and President Hugh E. Paine. One woman spat at him as he and his wife passed through the crowd. Pickets marched back and forth in front of the Manhattan headquarters. Eighteen Society members filed suit to oust the entire Board of Managers. Other members angrily resigned.

Hugh Paine and Society administrators faced a minority reaction to a new state law. The Metcalf-Hatch Law—a name unfortunate in its connotation of cattle breeding and poultry farm—authorizes approved laboratories and hospitals to requisition through the Department of Health unclaimed, unwanted animals from any humane organization receiving public funds. The Society receives public funds in the form of dog license fees. Therefore, the law obliges the Society to provide, on demand, unwanted animals for experimentation.

Cloudy thinkers among the vociferous minority harbored the idea that the Society itself had somehow invented Metcalf-Hatch. Which it had not. Nor had it supported the law. The Society had no hand in the matter; nor had it any choice. The law was specific, the Society had to obey it. That was that.

That was not quite that. The Society would obey the law —but Paine inaugurated a special policy: inspecting laboratories using animals in research. If the law forced the Society to give up unclaimed animals for experimentation, the Society determined to make sure the animals at least had proper care. While Metcalf-Hatch did not grant the right of inspection, every requisitioning laboratory accepted the Society's policy. The ASPCA drew up a set of standards assuring laboratory animals of balanced diet; well-lighted, well-ventilated and clean wards; adequate quarters; considerate attention; enough exercise; and, where surgery is involved, proper anesthesia and postoperative care. The New York State Society for Medical Research agreed to the Society's withholding of animals from any institution failing to meet these standards.

Starting in 1961, the Society's own graduate veterinarians, rather than its humane agents, began to make unannounced inspections which now average about 250 per year. Hospital directors have welcomed the veterinarians. Substandard lab conditions result mainly from lack of knowledge, and when a Society vet makes recommendations the hospital complies quickly. Sixty-three institutions are involved.

Not long ago, an ASPCA veterinarian brought one laboratory's attention to dirty, disorderly animal wards, uncovered food barrels, littered cages and a roach population that wasn't part of anybody's research program. Following the Society's suggestions, the lab improved so thoroughly that one ASPCA inspector later called it a "model of scientific endeavor."

Nevertheless, one small segment of New York's animal lovers, ignoring the Society's efforts to work within the law, nagged Paine throughout his four-year term (1952–1956). The misunderstanding continues, although tempers show signs of cooling.

In the whole touchy question of animal experimentation, perhaps the most lucid summary of today's attitude comes from William Rockefeller. In 1959, when Rockefeller presented the Society's Medal of Honor to Baker, the space-traveling squirrel monkey, the ASPCA President stressed that the award was given "as an expression of the ASPCA's awareness that it is time for the humane movement to record its realization that it is only through carefully controlled scientific research . . . that further progress to the mutual benefit of man and animal can be achieved."

Rockefeller has since added:

"Animals, as well as man, must on occasion be called on to accept risks, and indeed to make sacrifices, for the general good of the community which includes them both.

"At the same time, true to the humane purposes for which the ASPCA was founded . . . we insist that any experimentation be conducted under conditions that eliminate pain and suffering to the maximum extent consistent with the particular objective, and be limited to areas where proper authority has determined that benefit to the general welfare may be expected. . . ."

However vigorous their leadership, ASPCA presidents have only one pair of hands. Perhaps through kindly assistance by the spirit of Henry Bergh, the Society has consistently attracted other men and women of unique talent and dedication. W. H. Horton, General Manager from 1906 to 1930, was a superb administrator during a period of rebuilding and consolidation. The late Sydney H. Coleman, for 21 years Executive Vice-President until his retirement in 1952, received international praise as a leader in humane work. Born in Bellona, New York, a Ph.B. from Syracuse University, Chairman of the New York State Humane Agency's Legislative Committee, Coleman was instrumental in reaching an anti-cruelty agreement with the movie industry. He helped plan and direct the building of shelters in four New York boroughs, as well as the new Manhattan Hospital and Shelter.

Warren W. McSpadden, the Society's General Manager and Assistant Treasurer from 1952 until his death following a heart attack in 1959, was an honor graduate of the University of Texas, member of Phi Beta Kappa, an educator, a faculty member of Columbia University—and a man with apparently unlimited capacity for work. The Society still strives to reach McSpadden's goal, a humane slaughter bill for New York State.

The present Administrative Vice-President, ex-professor William Mapel, likes to picture the Society's reorganization in university terms. "We've got five main divisions now," says Mapel, "like the colleges of a university, each with its own dean."

The "dean" of Operations, a division responsible for the legwork and the shelter operations of the Society, is Arthur L. Amundsen, who joined the ASPCA in 1937 to take charge of horse-watering. Since then, Amundsen has traveled halfway around the world, studying humane work in other countries. During his most recent expedition, he gained information that helped organize the Sydney H. Coleman Animalport.

Mrs. George Fielding Eliot joined the ASPCA in 1950—specifically to aid in fund raising for the new Manhattan Shelter. Well-known radio personality and NBC's assistant director for women's programs, June Eliot, a chic, attractive woman, stayed on with the Society, and now is Director of Publications and Programs. Associated under Mrs. Eliot is a group of volunteer workers presided over for more than a decade by an enthusiast named Maude Hayman, who walked in one day and announced she was a new volunteer worker. Mrs. Hayman, wife of a Wall Street broker, had seen an ASPCA appeal poster in a Fifth Avenue bus. Under Mrs. Eliot's direction, the volunteers have worked on all sorts of affairs, including the annual Animal Kingdom Ball. Proceeds from these functions help underwrite such activities as the medical examinations and spaying service that are part of the Society's adoption program.

British-born, benevolent-looking Comptroller Thomas A.

Fegan, member of the Society since 1937, does not believe in the green eyeshade and the quill pen; he contemplates an automated system for accounting and data processing. Automation in his "college," Fegan estimates, could in the long run save the ASPCA several thousand dollars a year.

Another "dean," Dr. John E. Whitehead, a handsome young graduate of the University of Pennsylvania's School of Veterinary Medicine, joined the Society in 1954 and now directs the ASPCA Hospital and Clinic. Well known for his clinical work in the diseases of small animals, Dr. Whitehead is particularly interested in radiography and clinical pathology.

The Society's reorganization gives new prominence to the Humane Work Division—the Society's reason for existence and, until recently, the department most hampered by lack of facilities. Humane Work now is a separate "college" under West Pointer and retired army officer, Colonel Edmond M. Rowan, a soft-spoken war hero with a soldier's gift for infinite ingenuity. Rowan was chosen after nearly eighty prospects had been screened and more than a score had been interviewed.

"With these colleges and deans," Mapel says, "I guess I'm something like a university provost. Of course," he adds with a chuckle, "I'm also the so-and-so who has to cope with the deficit."

Appointed Administrative Vice-President in 1961—"liberated from the pasture to the doghouse" as he puts it—Mapel arrived in time to help direct the $60,000 hospital-expansion program. Also, under his guidance, the Society instituted a new system of budget control, and launched a personnel-management program in line with Rockefeller's policy of modern management techniques.

To the executive family in 1963 were added two other newcomers: Edward W. Simms and Edward I. Metcalf.

Simms, at forty-five a retired army lieutenant colonel with several years of personnel training, carries the title of Personnel Manager. Metcalf, forty and an Amherst graduate, brings to the Society ten years of executive experience in the broad field of public relations. His title is Director of Public Relations.

Another new venture—and another first in the humane movement—is the ASPCA Management Training Program. The big industrial corporations have been nurturing coveys of future executives for some time now. Rockefeller, head of his own firm's training program, sees the executive incubator as the best way the Society can get long-term assurance of competent management.

The humane movement is a special field demanding a temperament different from the typical business personality. Nobody goes into it to build a fortune. In an organization like the Society, management must be efficient—and something more, because the end product is, essentially, kindness. Humane work makes demands on the heart as well as on the head. The number of people able to meet those demands is limited.

Some of them already work for the Society, whose policy has always been to promote as much as possible from within. "We hold the top of the ladder open for anybody who wants to climb," Rockefeller says, and the Society encourages personnel to do it. Society employees may apply for the management training. If any of the 258 staff members want more education to help them do their jobs better, the Society will pay, depending on grades, all or part of the expenses.

To develop its executive reservoir, the Society now takes on a limited number of "administrative assistants" who receive six months of training in the five "colleges." The Society holds that good supervisors must know the problems as well as the duties of those who work under them. Matters of organization, budget control, law enforcement, and humane education occupy the major part of the indoctrination period, but all trainees spend days on ambulance and squad-car detail, on cruelty investigations, and on shelter and kennel routine. And—under Ryan—every administrative assistant learns from experience the swift, sure, .38-caliber way to put a horse out of its misery.

Appropriately, these administrative assistants are mature men—or will be by the time they're ready for administrative responsibility. In addition, the Society contacts fifty colleges of agriculture throughout the country and offers summer jobs to suitable junior students. With this experience, the student may well be interested enough to apply for training after his graduation.

Good executives cost money—frequently more than the ASPCA has. The Society makes no bones about seeking men whose livelihood does not depend entirely on salary. It's a respectable way of buying proved ability and maturity at bargain rates.

Money, indeed, has always been a headache for the ASPCA. Red-ink dollars are its greatest liability.

On the other hand, imagination and resourcefulness are the Society's biggest assets—plus a special attitude that distinguishes all ASPCA staff.

"We are engaged in a great work of mercy," Sydney Coleman once said. "It cannot be thought of as an ordinary job. It calls for something a little higher, a little nobler."

5

The Latin Lion Tamer

The Society's work has always been more than the white-collar variety. The story goes that Henry Bergh, in the late 1860's, stopped a wagon driver carting a load of sheep and calves. The animals had been ruthlessly jammed together, some dying, some with broken legs, gouged eyes, heads scraping against the turning wheels. When Bergh suggested at least some small measure of comfort for the animals, the driver and his assistant mockingly refused. Bergh, although dressed like a fashion plate, was a powerful, broad-shouldered man; he collared the driver and assistant and emphasized his suggestion by knocking their heads together.

Another time, when Bergh asked a horsecar driver to lighten an overloaded vehicle, the man threatened to punch him in the nose. Whereupon, Bergh seized the fellow by the seat of the pants and tossed him into a snowbank. In the dead of winter, in slush and ice, Bergh carried hay and water, and with his own hands helped fallen horses to their feet.

It has been some years since ASPCA operatives have felt constrained to seize anyone by the seat of the pants, or knock heads together. It is a tribute to the Society's success in improving the status of animals that the public has almost forgotten how bad things used to be. One small segment, unaware of the Society's activities, even tends to look on the prevention of cruelty as no longer really necessary—a harmless and not too demanding pursuit, somewhat akin to bird watching.

Such a man was Captain Ford, a prissy sort of individual with a pencil-line mustache, always nattily dressed and wearing, in addition, a carefully cultivated sunlamp tan. The Captain had been appointed to an administrative job at one of the local zoos and, as a result, liked to think of himself as a big game hunter. Somehow he managed to convey the impression that if he hadn't captured each of the zoo's inhabitants with his bare hands, he was nevertheless perfectly capable of doing so.

The Society had asked the Captain to deliver a series of lectures to the staff, hoping his experiences would be valuable and instructive. As things turned out, the Captain spent most of his time talking less about animals than about what the Society should be doing.

"You men," the Captain exhorted, "have got to get out into the real world. You've got to be willing to work, to sweat, to get your hands dirty! Now, when I was in Nairobi . . ."

His remarks had a condescending tone, not improved by his habit of bouncing up and down on his toes, an effect he believed, perhaps, lent some kind of military flair to his comments.

Ryan, sitting in the back of the lecture hall, turned indignantly to his friend Tom. "Do you hear that guy?" he asked. "He sounds like we were a bunch of old ladies. What does he think we do? Sit around all day and drink tea?"

Ryan himself is one of the last persons in the world anyone would mistake for an old lady. After the lecture, and still irritated, he decided to find out how much the Captain really knew about animals. Ryan made his way to the front of the hall where the Captain was now putting away his notes.

"Oh, there's something I wanted to ask," Ryan said innocently. "I heard that some animals, when you lasso them, run toward you."

"Is that what you heard?" asked the Captain.

"The cowboys say there's only three that you can really count on to back off a lariat."

"How interesting," said the Captain.

"Which ones would they be?" Ryan asked.

"Well . . ." the Captain hesitated, "that depends. Which ones did your cowboy informant tell you?"

"A horse, for one," said Ryan. "A steer, and a wild bear."

"Quite possible," said the Captain. "I really couldn't say one way or the other. My field is big game, you know. I never had much time for barnyard animals."

"Barnyard!" Ryan muttered as the Captain left. "I never heard of a wild bear living in a barnyard!"

The Captain evidently classified camels as barnyard animals, too, for one cold night he telephoned to advise that one of the zoo's camels had refused to go back into its stall.

"Put a bridle on him," Ryan said, "and just lead him like a horse."

"I tried that," said the Captain. "It doesn't work. He won't get up."

"You mean he's sitting down?"

"Lying down," the Captain corrected. He added, "On his side."

Ryan turned to Tom, who was also on duty that night. "We better break out the horse-sling. The Captain's going to need it."

"Why?" Tom asked. "Did he slip?"

"Not yet," Ryan said. "But you never can tell."

At the zoo, a light frost had already settled on the suffering camel. The Captain paced back and forth, beating his arms to keep warm.

"Oh, there you are, men," he said. "Now just give me a

hand here." He noticed the horse-sling. "You won't need that. We'll do it the right way, the way the Egyptians do it. I remember one day in Cairo . . ."

Waving his hands in the air, the Captain began shouting commands in Arabic. The camel opened one eye and through his lips made a sound more typical of the Bronx than the Near East.

"I don't give a damn what they do in Cairo," Ryan said. "This animal's sick and he's going to freeze to death if we don't get him out of here."

Disappointed at the camel's inability to understand simple Arabic, the Captain finally agreed to let Ryan and Tom use the sling. In fact, the Captain automatically appointed himself supervisor of camel-raising operations.

"You there," he ordered, "tighten that girth! Don't let that strap hang down! Buckle up the other side!"

"Captain," Ryan said quietly, "just let us handle it. Believe me, it's going to work better that way. You see, if we tightened up the girth and buckled the other side, we could get this camel off the ground all right. There's only one trouble. He'd be upside down."

The Captain continued to give helpful suggestions. In spite of them, Ryan and Tom got the camel indoors and bedded down in a corner of the stall.

"Thank you, men," the Captain said. "I'll carry on from here."

"You aren't going to leave him like that!" Ryan said. "He'll have pneumonia by the morning!"

"Naturally," said the Captain, "I intend to wrap some blankets around him."

"Blankets be damned!" Ryan snorted. "You've got the best blankets in the world all over the zoo."

The Captain gave him a puzzled look.

"Manure!" Ryan said. "It'll keep him warmer than anything else."

"*Manure?*" asked the Captain.

"You heard me," Ryan said. The ASPCA agents were already on their hands and knees, scrabbling at the floor of the stall. "Go cart some manure in here. I don't care whether it's horse, elephant or rhinoceros!"

For the next couple of hours, Ryan, Tom and the Captain hauled manure. The three men were soaked and reeking. The Captain's natty suit and overcoat looked as if it had been dragged through every barn in the state. But the camel was warm; he was also highly aromatic but unquestionably more comfortable than any of the humans.

The exhausted Captain sat down on the ground. "I ought to change my clothes," he said. "But at this point, I don't think it would make any difference. I might as well stay the rest of the night."

"Give him a quart of whiskey," Ryan ordered. "And you might take a shot yourself."

Ryan and Tom left the Captain in the stall, meditatively picking bits of straw from his hat. Considering the amount of straw, it would take him quite a while.

Next morning, the Captain telephoned to advise that the camel was on the mend. "Something else," he added, hesitatingly. "I want to thank you men. I mean, I didn't realize . . . some of the things I might have said the other day about getting your hands dirty . . ."

"Forget it," Ryan told him.

"Tell me one thing," the Captain asked. "Do you people always give your animals that treatment?"

"No," Ryan said, "only if they need it."

The Captain's camel made a full recovery. But in New York, not all zoo-type animals are in zoos. They occasionally appear on the street. Ryan, one day, was ordered to report to the theater district.

"What is it this time?" he asked. "Trained seals?"

"No," said the ASPCA dispatcher. "Lions. Twelve of them."

"All together or in small groups?"

"The last I heard," said the dispatcher, "they were in cages. For your sake," he called, as Ryan started out the door, "I hope they still are."

On one of the side streets of the theatrical section, Ryan did indeed find twelve lions, arranged neatly along the sidewalk. He also found one enraged truck driver and a brunette who would have been pretty were she not in the midst of hysterics.

"Lady," the truck driver was saying when Ryan drove up, "I got a hauling business, not a charity foundation. You want me to move them lions, you pay me in advance."

"Tonto! Imbecile!" screamed the brunette. "I am Carmela the Magnificent! I pay you twice when I get my vaudeville booking!"

"Just pay me once," the truck driver answered, "only do it now."

"But I tell you I have no money yet," Carmela the Magnificent cried. "And how can I get bookings without lions? I cannot take them to my hotel. Do you want me to leave them on the street?"

"Lady," the truck driver said, "I don't care if you hitch them together and pull a hansom cab through Central Park." He slammed the door and pulled away. Carmela the Magnificent caught sight of Ryan and threw her arms around him.

"You, *señor*, you are the one who must help me!"

When Ryan eventually disentangled himself, and Carmela the Magnificent had calmed down a little, he ascertained that the lions actually did belong to her; that she did have a vaudeville act but not right at the moment. Carmela the Magnificent showed him a theatre poster of herself, dressed in a gold-braided uniform and surrounded by her twelve performers. Ryan had heard of lady bullfighters and he saw no reason why there shouldn't be lady lion tamers as well. What he could do for the animals was something else again.

"I'll take them to the shelter," he said. "After that, we'll see."

The ASPCA has never been known to turn a deaf ear to the roaring of hungry lions—or, for that matter, the entreaties of a lady in distress. The Society agreed to house the animals rent-free until Carmela the Magnificent could book the act again. In addition, the Society offered to provide food free of charge. There was one stipulation. The ASPCA demands a great deal from its staff in the way of dedication and courage; nevertheless, it does not consider its employees expendable. Carmela the Magnificent would have to feed her own lions.

"But that is wonderful!" Carmela cried happily. "Of course I feed them. They will be no trouble. You will not even know they are there!"

Carmela the Magnificent exaggerated slightly. No one, not even the ASPCA staff, can hear a series of deep-throated roars without pausing to realize lions are in the vicinity. The dogs in the next-door kennels, born and raised New Yorkers, had never smelled lion in their lives. They did now and decided they didn't like it. They might have thought themselves back in Africa with some of their ancestors. Even the cats were a little uneasy, like children with distant relatives visiting.

The Latin lion tamer arrived daily to give her cast their meat rations. Her act included playing a guitar in the lions' cage. Carmela didn't try this at the Society but she always brought the instrument with her and spent some time strumming and crooning at the lions in Spanish. "They are so nice," she said, "just like little kitties. Even Metro."

Metro was the big, tawny male, the star of the show.

Carmelita had named him so because he looked, she said, like the movie trademark. "He is a little grumpy," she said, "but only in the morning."

Henry, the kennelman, was fascinated by Metro. "He's really great," he told Ryan. "Boy, I'd sure like to have him for a watchdog. Or on the subway with me."

"If Carmela the Magnificent doesn't get a booking soon," Ryan told Henry, "you may have to take him home with you. These lions can really eat."

"But that's good," Henry said. "It's a lot safer. It kills their appetite for things like people."

One morning Carmela the Magnificent failed to appear. Like hungry boarders, the lions turned restless and began to grumble. Noon came with still no sign of the lady lion tamer.

"I'll feed them," Henry volunteered.

"The hell you will," said Ryan. "Give her a little more time. If she doesn't show up, then we'll see what we can do."

Henry withdrew to the kennels. Ryan stayed in the adjoining room to direct owners who had brought their pets for veterinary examinations. The waiting room was crowded and busy. Some time passed before Ryan had the impression of a faint voice calling his name. It sounded as if it came from the kennels.

Ryan hurried to investigate. He found Henry at the far end of the kennel, his hand on the knob of the back door.

In the middle of the floor stood Metro, lashing his tail and looking curiously at Henry.

"I tried to feed him," Henry said faintly. "I did everything Carmela did. I just raised the cage door a little bit . . ."

"Why are you whispering?"

"You'd whisper too," Henry gulped, "if Metro looked at you the way he looked at me."

"Didn't you give him his food?" Ryan asked. "Put it in the cage. Maybe he'll go back and eat it."

"I did," Henry said. "He'd rather be out. I think I'll be leaving, too."

Ryan whipped out his .45 automatic.

"Don't shoot him," Henry pleaded. "He'll be all right once he's locked up."

"I'm not going to shoot him," Ryan said. "But if you try to go out that door I might make a mistake and shoot *you*. You stay here and help."

Ryan had seen lion tamers at work. He suddenly realized it felt different doing it yourself. He seized a pitchfork and held it at arm's length, the automatic in his other hand. "Metro!" he shouted with all the authority he could muster. "Metro! Back!"

The lion only gave him a disagreeable look.

Henry had stationed himself beside Metro's cage, and had raised the sliding door. "Maybe he doesn't understand English. Carmela always talks to him in Spanish. Try it. *Caramba! Mañana! Hasta la vista!*" Henry shouted.

Metro tossed his head angrily. Then he sat back on his haunches and roared.

"That's the wrong Spanish, maybe," Henry said.

"Just shut up," Ryan ordered. He took a firmer grip on the pitchfork and shook it at the lion. Metro pawed back at it. Ryan stepped closer. He filled his lungs with air.

"*Scat!*" he shouted at the top of his voice, aiming the revolver at the ceiling and pulling the trigger.

Metro sprang into the cage. Henry slammed the door and collapsed on the floor. The lion calmly began eating breakfast.

"Carmela said they were just like cats," Ryan murmured, wiping his dripping forehead. "I guess she was right."

Later in the day, Carmela finally arrived. She had wonderful news. An out-of-town theater had booked her act and she was sending a truck around immediately.

Ryan wished her luck. He mentioned nothing about Metro. Henry was still pale from the experience.

"Boy, I don't know how you did it," he admitted.

"The secret," Ryan said, "is never let the animal know you're scared."

"Oh yeah?" Henry said. "How come your hands are shaking?"

"That's what I mean," Ryan said. "I was scared, all right. But Metro never found out."

6

The Siberian Silver Dollar

The number of lions Ryan sees is relatively, and fortunately, small. Not so with horses. New York had 175,000 horses when Ryan started working for the Society. He began to suspect he would eventually meet every one of them. With other ASPCA agents, Ryan inspected horse markets, circuses, stockyards, ferry slips, and kept his eye on all street traffic. He also began to believe that horses possessed abilities even he had never realized. They could get themselves into as much trouble as a cat.

Manholes, especially open ones, seemed to have an irresistible attraction for horses. They fell into them. How so much horse could get into so little manhole baffled Ryan. But they did it. The latticework of the Queensboro Bridge held another fatal charm, particularly during the middle of the night in the dead of winter. Sewer catch basins appeared devised for the sole purpose of ensnaring a horse's leg.

A good part of Ryan's life took on the aspect of a battle of wits: between the horses, bent on discovering all the different ways of getting stuck in an infinite variety of urban pitfalls; and himself, urgently trying to discover the best way of getting them out.

He developed, in the course of the battle, several basic techniques. The Anti-Catch-Basin Technique was one. When a horse's leg slipped through the slot of the catch basin, the animal was usually caught permanently. Hoof and leg seemed to go through the slot with amazing ease; but what goes in does not necessarily come out and the horse might just as well have fallen into an unopenable trap. In those cases, Ryan assumed the role of a blacksmith. Crouched at ground level, contorted in a way that would have amazed any ordinary blacksmith, Ryan very carefully slipped his hands down and removed the shoe from the captive hoof. Then, with a sharp knife, he painstakingly whittled the hoof until it could pass freely through the slot.

The Anti-Manhole Technique was less intricate but could involve more equipment. Its principles, however, were simple and direct:

1. Grease the manhole
2. Grease the horse
3. Pull out the horse

This usually did the job; if it didn't, Ryan could put the Society's horse-derrick into action. The horse-derrick was a combination of ropes, pulleys, winches, slings and a supporting base. It resembled some ancient Roman siege machine but could lift a horse to its feet more efficiently than half a dozen men.

But horses not only got stuck; they got sick. The Society presently has a staff of fourteen veterinarians and a research laboratory as complete as a good many hospital facilities. The Society had only a limited number of veterinarians in the earlier days, and its agents were often looked on as authorities in the treatment of animals. Ryan in particular found himself handing out practical suggestions, especially in the poorer neighborhoods. New York's immigrants seemed terrified of doctors in any form. A doctor meant money. Calling a doctor also had a frightening formality about it; and, like telegrams with bad news, the immigrants associated doctors with catastrophe. They would rather dose themselves and their animals with patent medicines, weird home brews and violent liniments than think about calling a doctor or veterinarian. With Ryan, however, they felt more at ease. And Ryan often felt that, in addition to preventing cruelty, he was running a mobile consulting clinic.

On Manhattan's lower East Side, his regular patients included a horse belonging to Vadim Sergeivich Orlovsky. Vadim Sergeivich was a man of mystery. He wore a tall woolly Cossack cap, a Russian-style blouse belted outside his trousers, a pair of cracked boots. Vadim Sergeivich had been a high-ranking officer during the Russo-Japanese War, had defended Port Arthur almost single-handed, conducted glittering affairs with countesses, fought duels, defeated attacking wolves. All of this was obviously true, because confirmation of his stories came from an indisputable authority, Vadim Sergeivich himself.

"It is I, Vadim Sergeivich Orlovsky, who speaks!" the Russian would cry, which had the effect of putting an end to any further discussion.

In New York, Vadim Sergeivich occupied himself with the refreshment business. That is, he drove a delivery wagon loaded with seltzer-water siphons. It would do until something more appropriate turned up.

That it would turn up, Vadim Sergeivich had no doubt. His assurance came from an object he carried with him at all times, tucked away under his baggy blouse. Although taking it out of its hiding place required the Russian practically to undress, he was always happy to do so. Then he would hold his lucky piece triumphantly between thumb and forefinger.

"With this," he would say, "I have nothing to fear, my family shall never beg from any man. Take my word for it. It is I, Vadim Sergeivich Orlovsky, who tells you these things!"

The object was an American silver dollar. Its milled edge looked brand new, the profile of Liberty clear and sharp; but the dollar was jet black. Orlovsky had acquired it during one of his Russian adventures. Exactly how or where he would not reveal. He would wink eloquently and return the piece to its hiding place.

Of the entire Orlovsky household, Vadim, his wife, son and horse, the most essential member was the horse. Orlovsky never admitted this. He preferred to imply that somewhere a whole stableful of horses stood at his disposal. Ryan knew otherwise. If anything happened to Orlovsky's horse, the Russian simply could not afford to replace it. He would automatically be out of the seltzer business.

The charm of the silver dollar might have extended to Vadim Sergeivich's wife and son; it did not have any noticeable power as far as the horse was concerned. The animal fell into manholes, drainage ditches, and sewer basins with monotonous regularity; potholes had a magnetic effect. The horse also showed a genuis for seeking out loose paving blocks to stumble over. On a sunny day, the horse could even manage to trip on its own shadow. And it was Ryan who always raced to the scene, putting the animal back on its feet and Vadim Sergeivich back in business.

"I'll be damned if I've ever seen a horse like that," Ryan told the Russian. "I don't know where you got him, but he's no city horse. I just don't think he understands the city."

"He will learn," Orlovsky said confidently.

Ryan held the opinion that, considering the horse's age, if he hadn't learned by now the prospects were dim. Some horses could get along in Manhattan. Some couldn't. Ryan was convinced that Orlovsky's horse would never fathom the mysteries of manholes and how to avoid them. Once or twice, he suggested that Orlovsky trade the animal to a farmer and get himself a more sophisticated one, but the Russian only grunted.

Meanwhile, the horse continued to pull the seltzer-bottle wagon, with time out for his routine entanglements with the manholes and catch basins. One afternoon, however, Ryan had a frantic message from Orlovsky. The animal had collapsed at a ferry slip.

Ryan and one of the Society's veterinarians hurried to the river. Orlovsky's horse lay on its side, flanks heaving, eyes glassy. The seltzer-bottle wagon stood near the curb, its shafts empty. The vet examined the animal, then stood up and shook his head. The horse's hindquarters were paralyzed.

"There's nothing anybody can do," the vet said to Ryan. "That horse is done. I think you'll have to shoot it. It's a damn shame."

Orlovsky's face had turned gray. He said nothing.

"Wait a minute," Ryan said. "Let me try something."

"You're wasting your time," the vet said. "Even suppose you keep the poor devil alive. What's the use if he's going to be paralyzed?"

"I'll worry about that later," said Ryan. "Come on, give me a hand."

Together, the men got a sling on the horse and hoisted it into the ambulance and headed back to the shelter's stables. Orlovsky offered to come along but Ryan waved him back. "I'll handle this alone."

"Well, I'll try . . ." the vet began.

"No thanks, Doc." Ryan shook his head. "This is between the horse and me."

Ryan set up his own operating room on the stable floor. For the rest of the day and far into the night, Ryan worked over the animal. The horse, Ryan realized, was toxic; he tried every method he knew to fight it. Working alone, in the narrow stall under the hard light of an electric bulb, Ryan practically readjusted the animal's entire body chemistry.

Past midnight, there was no sign of improvement. By three in the morning, Ryan began to consider the possibility that the veterinarian might have known more than he did.

Then he put the vet out of his thoughts and went wearily back to the animal. As he had said, this was between Orlovsky's horse and himself.

A little before dawn, Ryan had to admit that even he had done all he could. He leaned back against the wooden partition and waited.

In another hour, the horse stirred feebly; then, as Ryan watched, the animal struggled to its feet and whinnied. Since there were no manholes for the horse to fall into at the moment, Ryan decided it was safe to sleep. Without moving from the stall, he sighed with relief and closed his eyes.

Vadim Sergeivich showed up at the stable around daybreak. He, too, had been working through the night. At first, he had tried pulling the wagon himself. Failing, he had carried the load case by case on his back until he had finished his deliveries. When Ryan saw him, he was looking worse than the horse.

As much as Orlovsky had disbelieved the animal would have to be destroyed, he now could not believe the horse was alive. When he finally understood, he tossed his Cossack hat in the air and threw his arms around Ryan.

"There is only one truth," he cried. "The difference between life and death! I, Vadim Sergeivich Orlovsky, tell you this!"

His face fell when Ryan regretfully told him the other part of the story. The horse was alive, but the paralysis had left its mark. The animal was sound and well—with one exception. It could pull a load forward, but would never again have the strength to back one up. It could change directions only by going in a wide circle.

"But in the city is impossible," Orlovsky said in dismay. "For a cart horse not to back up . . . the narrow streets, the corners, all the traffic . . ."

"I thought about that," Ryan said. "I'll see what I can do."

Later in the day, Ryan embarked on a three-sided horse trade. It involved Orlovsky, an iceman and a farmer.

Ice-wagon horses, Ryan knew, worked terrifically hard. By the end of one season they were nearly worn out. Compared to hauling blocks of ice, pulling a load of seltzer bottles was a rest cure. On this basis, he set about finding an iceman interested in a fresh animal. Farm horses were strong enough to pull ice wagons, so Ryan also needed to locate a farmer willing to trade. Then, of course, he had to find a place for Orlovsky's horse. Juggling all these factors and requirements, Ryan consummated a very delicate deal. Through a series of tradings and counter-tradings, he acquired an ice-wagon horse for Orlovsky's seltzer-bottle wagon; he discovered an iceman delighted to have a farm horse; and he contacted a farmer just outside the city who would be very glad to use Orlovsky's horse for plowing—an occupation that didn't require any backing up.

Orlovsky shook his head in amazement. It was probably the only horse trade in Manhattan that left everybody satisfied.

"What can I do?" Orlovsky asked. "What can I say? For this words are not enough."

"You can do one thing," Ryan said. "Tell me how, in the name of geography, you got hold of an American silver dollar in Russia!"

"Ah, that," Orlovsky said with a shrug. "That is one story I do not know. I found it.

"You give me my horse's life," he went on, "you give me back my living. I give you truth in exchange. It is true I was in war. But not officer. Only private. I did not even fight. I guarded camp in Siberia. There I found the dollar, lying on ground, as black as it is now. How it came or why, I do not know.

"But I know this," Vadim Sergeivich said. "When I found this dollar from America I decided I would go there. And I kept it with me all through war. It was like I had America in my pocket."

The Russian reached under his blouse and took out the coin. He handed it to Ryan.

"Here," Vadim Sergeivich said, "it is yours. I am in America now, I have no need of it. For luck . . ." The Russian nodded. "There is only luck we make for ourselves, or the luck a good friend gives us. I, Vadim Sergeivich Orlovsky, tell you this. Of course," he added, "as long as you carry it, you can never say you are without a dollar."

The ice-wagon horse gained weight on the seltzer route. Orlovsky's horse took to farming as if born to the job. In the fields, there were no manholes, no sewer gratings to distract it. The last Ryan heard, the horse was doing well. Even if it did trip over a clod now and then.

The Society has always worked to prevent abuse to New York's draft animals. As part of the effort, it set up fountains and watering troughs throughout the city. One year, when the municipal authorities ordered all fountains shut down during a glanders epidemic, the Society organized a drinking-pail service. Later, the organization bought some surplus watering carts and made mobile oases of them by outfitting the street-sprinkling equipment into faucets for filling pails; the ASPCA had also increased the number of permanent watering stations to 70.

During one year alone, the ASPCA examined nearly 23,000 horses at auction sales. It routinely checked conditions in all stables; but one thing the Society could foresee, warn against, and do little to prevent, was fire. Even the best-run stables were fire hazards; and some of the ramshackle barns and livery stables at the fringes of the city were tinder-boxes. Because of the constant danger of fire, and the large number of animals that might be threatened, the ASPCA set up a direct line with the city's fire-prevention bureau.

Fires, like children, seem to be born in the small hours of the morning. Ryan got used to having his sleep interrupted and, when animals were in danger, he usually hustled to the scene as fast as the fire engines. The ASPCA horse ambulance generally arrived ahead of the hospital vehicles, too—a situation which made some of the hospital administrators wonder whether the ASPCA had extrasensory perception or whether the Society's drivers had some secret underground passages below the streets of Manhattan.

During one of the coldest winters New York had known, Ryan tumbled out of bed to drive frantically to a burning stable. There were 76 horses in the building, but the fire department had the blaze under control and Ryan got them out with no difficulties—other than those inherent in manipulating 76 terrified animals.

While the firemen struggled with freezing equipment, and the police stamped their feet in the wistful hope of avoiding frostbite, Ryan tethered the horses along the street.

"You're lucky," a shivering policeman told him, "you can go back to bed."

"Bed hell!" Ryan said. "I haven't even started this job."

"You got the horses out," said the policeman, through chattering teeth.

"Oh, sure," Ryan said. "I got them out. Now what do you think I'm going to do with them? Let them take a walk in the park? They'll catch pneumonia if they stand out here any more."

"So will I," said the policeman. "But I'm doing it anyway."

"You have to," said Ryan. "They don't."

The policeman was in no mood for worrying about horses. "Why don't you just knit them some jackets? Maybe some little booties to match."

"I think I can do better than that," said Ryan. He had noticed a quilt factory next to the stable. "Do me a favor, will you? Just break down that door a little bit."

"Oh, no," the policeman said. "You aren't going to take them animals in there."

"I want some quilts," Ryan said. "I need seventy-six big quilts. They'll be as good as blankets."

"Quilts!" shouted the policeman. "Why don't you get some feather beds while you're at it? You know we can't go breaking into private property."

"If that quilt factory was burning," Ryan said, "you'd break in, wouldn't you?"

The policeman gave Ryan a strange look. It crossed his mind that Ryan was perhaps capable of setting fire to the building just to get his seventy-six quilts. "Look," the policeman said, "there's an emergency phone number on the door. If you're going to smash a man's factory and take off with his merchandise, the polite thing would be to sort of tell him about it ahead of time. It's a small courtesy, I know. But people appreciate it. You'd be surprised."

The policeman promised to phone the owner. "Tell him it's an emergency," Ryan called. "And tell him it's too damned cold out here to wait around."

By the time the policeman came back, Ryan had already put his shoulder to the door and was rummaging around a pile of quilts.

"He says it's all right," the officer advised. "He says he never heard of anybody wrapping up horses in quilts. But if that's what you want, go ahead."

All the quilts Ryan found were too small. One quilt would barely cover half a horse. Two per animal, he decided, would be just right. On a worktable, he discovered a heavy needle and some pack thread. Pulling the quilts into a pile, Ryan squatted down in the midst of it and began to sew.

"You know, Ryan," said the policeman, "you'd make one hell of a leprechaun."

"Don't waste time talking," Ryan muttered, his mouth full of thread. "Just get sewing."

In a little while, Ryan had transformed the pile of quilts into suitable horse covers. "Now all we need to do is get the horses to the shelter."

"We?" asked the policeman.

"Do you want them galloping all over New York?" Ryan asked.

New Yorkers are used to odd sights and take pride in not being startled by them. But even the most blasé New Yorker would have been mildly surprised at Ryan's cavalcade that night. Marching ahead, lantern in hand, Ryan shouted orders to a squad of blue-coated policemen, reinforced by a hastily recruited contingent of Skid Row residents, trying to keep seventy-six horses in line. The horses wore the quilts Ryan had stitched together and the ensembles were most attractive: floral patterns, entwined roses, acanthus leaves in a variety of colors, reminiscent of the Easter Parade.

At the ASPCA shelter, Ryan parked horses wherever he could find room. He filled the stalls with horses. He drove the Society's trucks into the street and filled the garage with horses. He made room in the kennels for horses. The only thing that kept him from filling up the offices and lavatories was that he eventually ran out of horses.

Then he went to a bar.

"Whiskey!" Ryan ordered. His face by this time had acquired alternating layers of soot and ice.

The bartender took down a bottle and began pouring a shot.

"No, no," Ryan said. "More!"

"A double?" the bartender asked.

"More than that," Ryan cried. "Man, I need a *case* of whiskey!"

He carried the whiskey back to the shelter and dosed each horse. Later in the morning, after the animals had been sorted out and checked over, Ryan sat down to catch his breath.

"It's amazing," said one of the Society's veterinarians. "Those horses are in perfect shape. But I wish I'd seen the expression on that bartender's face."

"It didn't surprise him," Ryan said. "I guess I looked like I needed a drink. The only thing he wanted to know was: should he wrap up the case of whiskey or did I want to drink it there?"

Ryan needed no whiskey one night in midsummer. What he needed most he could not get: time. On Charles Street that night, fire had swept a big stable so quickly that it was practically an instant ruin. The damage was to reach a quarter of a million dollars.

"We're licked," the fire chief told Ryan. "It's gone too fast. If we had every hook and ladder in New York it wouldn't do us any good."

"How many horses are in there?" Ryan asked.

"About seventy. They're all dead. Burned or suffocated."

"What do you mean dead?" Ryan shouted. "My God, man, I can hear them in there screaming."

"That's on the second floor," said the fire chief. "But they're done for, too. We can't get near them. You might as well forget it—"

Before the chief could say any more, Ryan had dashed across the fire lines into the burning stable. The chief had been right. Blackened bodies of horses filled the first floor. The ramps and stairways to the second floor had been burned away. Overhead, Ryan could hear the cries of the animals still alive.

The heat forced Ryan outside again. Next door to the stable was a one-story building the flames had not quite demolished.

"Get some men over here with a ladder," shouted Ryan. When it came, he clambered up to the low roof. Through a window at one end of the stable, Ryan saw about fifty horses milling inside.

"I need a ramp," Ryan called. "Get me a ramp and I'll bring out every one of them."

"No good!" the chief shouted back. "That roof's going to go. If the fire doesn't get them, the smoke will."

"There's two big windows," Ryan said, "and a skylight. Smash them in. Those horses will suffocate if you don't.'

"Fresh air won't get them out."

"No," Ryan said, "but it'll keep them alive till *I* do."

Ryan, who had been a custom tailor for horses during the winter, now became an architect. The chief dispatched what men he could spare to help Ryan haul up some beams from a subway construction in the next block. Throughout the dawn and early morning, the sweating men shored up the roof and built a makeshift ramp.

Ryan gritted his teeth and climbed to the top of the building again. One by one through the smashed window, he led the horses across the roof, down the ramp to the street.

By late afternoon, Ryan was back at the ASPCA headquarters. He looked at his watch.

"Five o'clock," Ryan said with surprise. "I guess it's time to call it a day."

He had spent fifteen hours at the fire. He had rescued fifty-one horses.

The Society awarded Ryan its Distinguished Service Medal for those fifteen hours. No one doubted he deserved it—including the fire chief.

"But you know, Ryan," the chief told him later, "I can't figure why I listened to you when you told me to smash in the skylight and those windows. Making a draft like that's against every rule of fire fighting. You're OK with horses," the chief added. "But you sure don't know a damned thing about being a fireman."

7

The Friendly Persuaders

Ryan admits he would never have made a good fire fighter, and prefers his official title: "Inspector and Training Instructor." As such, he is attached to the heart of Society operations, the Humane Work Division. Since its founding, the ASPCA has undertaken dozens of humane activities, even sponsoring pet shows. But the public sees only the more obvious examples: the Perils-of-Pauline rescue of a cat from a window ledge; the puppies and kittens in the adoption wards; the hospital, the shelters. For a good many people, "Be Kind to Animals" is a hand-embroidered platitude in the category of "Home Sweet Home"; or one of those commendable yet nebulous ideas like the Fourth Dimension. For the Humane Work Division, prevention of cruelty is the reason for its existence, a 24-hour-a-day, year-round job. It leads to some strange places.

One such was a ripe, rat-infested dump in Long Island's Moriches Bay area. Reports had come in that the spot swarmed with tiny ducklings. Shocked by the complaints, hardly believing anybody would toss out live poultry with rubbish, Arthur L. Amundsen, present Director of Operations, hurried to check on it himself.

The reports were true. "This is one of the cruelest things I've ever seen," Amundsen says. "Dozens of ducklings with broken or twisted legs, maimed, burned, half eaten by rats, or starved to death."

Amundsen and Society agents found ducklings dragged into rat holes or trapped under cans, bottles and heaps of trash. Despite the blistering midsummer sun, many of the tiny creatures had managed to survive.

The agents collected 30 or 40 ducklings and transported them to the shelter; scores of others, crippled or burned beyond help, had to be humanely destroyed.

Commercial duck raisers, the Society learned, had been dumping barrels of surplus eggs. In the warmth of the sun and the smoldering trash fires, fertile eggs soon hatched. The little ducks emerged not into a brave new world of water and green grass but a nightmare. An incubator, the dump was also a death trap.

The farmers themselves could have spared the unhatched ducklings this torment by taking a few minutes to break the eggs they intended to discard; or to let them stand briefly in cold water. When the Society asked for cooperation, the growers agreed. But the following season, the egg dumping continued.

Although Society agents, as peace officers, have authority to make arrests and issue summonses, no agent may sign a complaint on his own unless he personally witnesses an act of cruelty. Nobody from the Society had, so far, actually seen farmers throwing out fertile eggs. For weeks, agents patrolled the area. It was not a pleasant assignment.

Finally, one of the Society people caught a grower dumping barrels of eggs in varying stages of hatching. Along with the eggs were 13 live and peeping baby ducks.

This was the on-the-spot evidence the Society required to go to court. It was an open-and-shut case of cruelty. Even the defense attorney suggested the need for an ordinance against disposing of eggs at a public dump. Township authorities acted quickly, passing a local law carrying a fine and jail sentence for violators.

At the trial, the ducklings were star witnesses. Later,

Amundsen himself adopted a number of them. Under his care, they grew large and sleek; they tramped happily around the Amundsen garden, quacking as well as if they had been born on a model farm instead of a desolate dump.

Far from Long Island's duck farms, the New York waterfront has figured in the Society's humane work, although in this case, it wasn't a matter of investigating deliberate cruelty, but, in a sense, carrying a small flag of truce in a labor-management dispute.

On the eve of a shipping strike, a stevedore telephoned the Society about a special problem.

"We're going off the job," he advised. "And that's OK with me. But it won't be OK with the cats around here."

Some of Manhattan's cats have chosen to follow careers on the waterfront. They leave the hard work of loading and unloading to the dockhands but help out by keeping down the rat population. Stevedores are tough characters; so are the portside cats, and the two groups get along splendidly. The stevedores share their lunches with the cats and make sure there's food left for them.

The strike, leaving the waterfront deserted, threatened the cats with loss of their daily rations. The Society contacted shipping offices in the area and a night watchman agreed to feed the animals.

The cats weathered the strike and, as soon as it was settled, went back to sharing the stevedores' ham sandwiches. Cats are notoriously indifferent to disputes between humans, but in this case the stevedores judged the cats' sympathies to be with the union. Throughout the strike, no cat ever crossed a picket line.

The stevedore had the right idea. He wanted to stop a bad situation before it started and the Society wishes more people would think along those lines. Animals, just as humans, have well-defined legal safeguards and the Society will protect a mistreated animal to the limit, using, if necessary, all the machinery the law provides. But it has never assumed the attitude of an avenging angel, smiting the wicked in its wrath. The Humane Work Division's basic aim is not to punish but prevent cruelty.

To achieve this, the Division makes more than 8,000 inspections a year. Special agents attend every performance and rehearsal of circuses and rodeos, every official horse show within a 65-mile radius of Columbus Circle; they check circuses and rodeos, race tracks, poultry markets, riding academies, kennels, zoos, pet shops, stockyards and slaughterhouses.

These last two, in Bergh's time, ranked among the worst offenders. Through the Society's constant efforts, most meat processors today have learned that humane treatment pays off in safer, more efficient operations, less waste and a better product. The Federal Government recognizes this, too, and meat packers selling directly or indirectly to the government must abide by the federal humane slaughter legislation passed in 1960. This covers about 90 percent of meat bought in the United States, and 480 federally inspected establishments. The smaller packers that don't sell to the government aren't obliged to install humane slaughtering methods unless state laws require them to do so. (Fifteen states have already passed legislation of this type. New York, usually a leader in such matters, is not one of them and the Society still presses for a humane slaughter law.)

If the Society finds a violation—or potential violation—in any of the places it inspects, an agent explains the situation carefully to the person responsible and suggests ways of correcting it. Most people willingly cooperate. In flagrant, persistent or deliberate violations, the Society has authority to bring the offender to court.

On top of the continual inspections, the Society investigates more than 5,000 alleged cases of cruelty each year—an average of 15 per day. Until recently, it had to perform this task with a frantically overworked staff operating from a crowded cubicle at the Manhattan Shelter. The reorganization and expansion program gave the Division more room to turn around in and some more personnel to carry out the anti-cruelty activities.

Director of the Division is the sandy-haired, six-foot Colonel Rowan. The much-decorated Colonel's quick smile shows a certain optimism and indefatigability—and he needs every bit of it.

Rowan keeps on the go as much as his men, hurrying out to check on an investigation in Upstate New York, driving back again that night to follow up another one in Manhattan. Rowan insists on being at the scene in case of emergencies —an attitude which costs him numerous nights of sleep.

New York State laws relating to cruelty to animals are among the best if not the best animal laws in the country. Nevertheless, Colonel Rowan and his agents frequently run into legal snarls of varying magnitude. One law which perennially raises a storm of protests to the Society has to do with "set tails" on gaited show horses.

It has been the vogue for these gaited animals to sport tails that arch up abruptly from the hindquarters and cascade or fly in the breeze, sometimes with benefit of artificial lengthening and thickening. Producing the desired set-tail effect comes from an operation which severs certain muscles. Handlers maintain the artificial arch by keeping the horse's tail in a "bustle" a large part of the time it isn't in the show ring.

For many years large groups have sought to outlaw the practice of tail cutting and the showing of horses so treated. It's against the law in New York to perform this operation unless the owner can produce a veterinarian's certificate that the operation is necessary for the health or life of the creature. It also is against the law to show such an animal without the same veterinarian's affidavit.

Once the set-tail law became part of the New York State

code the ASPCA set out to enforce it. A large-scale rhubarb ensued, and some members of the ASPCA Board of Managers resigned.

Then came the stumbling block not known to the public in general. Because many horses with set tails are imported from outside New York, the New York statute was on two occasions held to violate the commerce clause of the United States Constitution. The latter of these court findings came in August of 1962. As a result, the law is unenforceable; but the tirade against the ASPCA continues.

Currently the Society is seeking some way out of this predicament. Conceivably an enforceable law will come. Getting around the interstate commerce angle is a poser, however. Possibly horse show officials all over the country may be persuaded—even if a moratorium of several years is necessary to permit existing valuable animals with set tails to pass into retirement—to show gaited horses the way God made them.

Time will tell. Meanwhile, the ASPCA has been advised that summonses issued under the present law will be thrown out of court.

Special agents under Rowan's supervision total 15, plus 2 inspectors and a Deputy Director. At one time, agents had to report back to the Manhattan Shelter no matter how far afield their investigations led them. Now, among the many other efficiencies Rowan has implemented, the agents work as flying squads or rotating teams; during any given assignment, they make the nearest ASPCA shelter their temporary headquarters. It has saved considerable shuttling back and forth through overcrowded New York and the agents can get onto their cases faster than ever before. They also telephone their office hourly and, in emergencies, the agent closest to the scene investigates immediately.

In addition to the New York City staff, volunteer agents

help the Society cover the entire state. These volunteers make on-the-spot investigations in the outlying areas; the Society follows up if the situation so requires.

One of these volunteers alerted the Society to one of its most distressing cases in several years: neglected livestock on a dairy farm in Upstate New York. From the road, the big, rambling buildings appeared well kept. But inside the reeking, encrusted barns, the Society found 75 starved, dead or dying Jersey cows and their calves.

The owner and her assistant, both of them elderly women in grimy, spattered housedresses, lived in the decaying farmhouse.

"It's so lovely here," murmured the assistant. "A beautiful, happy place. And the animals are so happy, too."

"My God," whispered an agent to the Society veterinarian who had driven up to check over the cattle, "she's looking right at a dead calf."

The veterinarian shook his head. "Some people only see what they want to see. The picture in her mind is a lot prettier than the one in front of her. No wonder she likes it better."

"But the owner . . ." the agent began. "Can't she see for herself?"

The vet turned away. "Didn't you notice?" he asked. "She's blind."

For months, the Society learned, the farm had been falling into ruin. Unpaid, the hired hands had drifted away one by one. The Society spent almost $1,000 bringing in fodder for the remaining animals and cleaning the stalls. The demented woman still refused to admit anything was amiss and even nailed up the barns to keep Society workers out.

To protect the cattle from slow death, the Society had no choice but to bring the case to court. One of the women was eventually committed to a mental institution. With the help of the Society, the cattle were fed and watered regularly; they recovered their health and were sold to a farm that could assure them adequate care.

Deplorable as it is, cruelty following in the wake of human breakdown shocks us a little less than deliberate mistreatment. Of all the strange byways the Society has followed in its efforts to protect animals, the strangest has been the human mind itself. Sadists and psychopathic killers find their victims among animals as often as among humans. Angry, vengeful, filled with hatred for themselves and everyone else, some men and women lash out at animals because the animal can't strike back. Only a psychiatrist could unravel the the motives of a 200-pound giant of a man who calmly beat a kitten to death with a rake. Or another man who stabbed his own wire-haired terrier with a pocket knife and left her to die in a trash can. And, tragically, some of the cruelest tormentors of animals are children.

"I couldn't begin to count the cases where adults and children, too, have tortured animals for amusement," says George Tuscher, present District Manager of the Queens Shelter and Supervisor of the Society's Humane Work Division from 1952 to 1961. "I remember plenty of it—and I wish I could forget."

In the overall picture, fortunately, pathological cruelty is relatively low on the list. Just as often, the Society man will run into a situation such as the following:

The ASPCA agent had gone out to investigate a complaint by a Brooklyn woman.

"That dog in the next building," she said, "they must be killing him. You can hear him all down the block."

The agent agreed that, from the sound of it, the dog must be having the hide peeled off him. The agent found the apartment easily and a pin-curled woman came to the door. The Society man questioned her very politely and carefully while the dog, sitting on the divan, yowled and howled relentlessly.

"What's wrong with the dog?" she asked indignantly. "There's nothing wrong." She invited the agent in to see for himself. "Am I cruel?" she cried. "I'm not even touching him. He just likes to bark!"

The agent advised the neighbor that barking dogs are outside the Society's jurisdiction—unless, of course, the dog is barking because of provable cruelty. Many people believe that anything involving animals is a case for the Society. It isn't true. With compulsive barkers, the best the Society can do is suggest that the disturbed neighbor call the police or health departments—and offer sympathy.

Among the easiest cases to correct are those of unwitting, unintentional cruelty: in shops where an uninformed salesgirl neglects to check the cleanliness of water in a fish tank; the man who believes a whip will teach his dog obedience; enthusiastic young biologists who seriously believe they aid the cause of science by experimenting on a neighborhood cat. A warning usually suffices, and often the offender is amazed to realize he has been heedlessly cruel.

The ASPCA follows up all such cases to make sure they really are corrected. If not, the Society will prosecute. But it's seldom necessary to go that far. Of all the cases the Society investigates in a year, only about 1 percent calls for court action.

The toughest and most disheartening cases of cruelty are those resulting from a type of blind egotism—a complete disinterest and disregard for an animal's suffering. One woman, taking an extended vacation, left her two dogs locked up at home without food or water. A Bronx peddler drove his horse through the streets, unconcerned that the animal had no shoes. Stable-owners (who, of all people, should know better) continue to rent out animals covered with saddle sores. During a TV broadcast, a magician tried to hypnotize a rabbit. But the rabbit, evidently having a stronger mentality than the hypnotist, didn't cooperate. The magician seized the rabbit by the ears and slammed it down repeatedly against the table. Explaining his treatment of the animal, the magician only shrugged and commented: "She wasn't working so good. I don't know why. Maybe because she's pregnant."

The magician is an exception. In a business hardly noted for calm reserve or avoidance of the spectacular, most show people with animal acts take reasonable care of their performers. It would be pleasant to think that show people are more tenderhearted than others—and perhaps they are; even so, a trained animal is valuable property, the owner's bread and butter, and the showman has a certain deep personal interest in protecting it.

At the same time, the mental processes of entertainment producers or publicity agents are not always susceptible to analysis. One radio station hinted that a white bird might be the clue to finding a hidden $1,000 bill. New Yorkers, tending to take things literally, descended on City Hall Park en masse, armed with nets. The Society had to send a truck and four agents to protect the birds, and even at that, many pigeons were injured—some of them weren't even white.

One TV director, the Society learned, planned to squirt ammonia into a dog's face, presumably to bring out some subtle emotion not obtainable otherwise. The Society contacted a program representative who agreed to drop this bit of business. "I regret to say," apologized the flustered representative, "that not one of us was aware that the ammonia spray could prove harmful to dogs."

The National Association of Radio and Television Broadcasters' code includes this passage:

> The use of animals, both in the production of television programs and as a part of television program content, shall at all times be in conformity with accepted standards of humane treatment.

With this assurance, the Society can only keep its fingers crossed—and hope that some TV writer doesn't come up with a scene requiring an elephant on water skis.

Theater people are probably smartest when it comes to animals. They avoid them. Directors shy away from using animals as props. Unless you twist his arm, an actor will shun playing a scene with a dog or cat on the stage. First, nobody can predict how the animal will behave. Besides, a dog or cat will upstage an actor every time.

"About half the complaints we get," says Colonel Rowan, "come from anonymous callers." Although shocked by a man beating his dog, the person who complains often feels vaguely embarrassed, or a little silly going to all that fuss over an animal. Perhaps the emergence of our better natures startles us, and we don't want to let on that anything has touched our sympathies. The desire not to stir up trouble, not to get involved, comes into play, too. In close-knit neighborhoods, people fear being known as talebearers and refuse, at the last moment, to sign a complaint or appear as a witness.

These very human attitudes make the Humane Work Division's job much tougher. At the same time, suddenly and unexpectedly, the public can go all out in backing up the Society. The judge in one highly publicized case, for example, was deluged with mail from animal lovers. Another time, the owner of a riding academy, accused of starving his horses, got bushels of indignant letters. "Someday," Rowan says, "we hope the public will be as quick to report cases of cruelty as it is to turn in a fire alarm.

"When we investigate an anonymous report of cruelty," Rowan adds, "we tread carefully. If the plantiff is unidentified and absent, by the same token the defendant doesn't know he's been accused." The Society is scrupulous about pointing out the legal position of all concerned—including the animal's. When working outside the New York City area, the Society makes sure to advise state police, local police and local humane associations.

Every case demands careful observance of the law and, usually, plenty of tact. Especially since the Society doesn't know in advance what it may run into. One night, Ryan went out to check a report of a scheduled fight between a dog and a badger.

The address was a Sutton Place penthouse. Another Society agent and a city detective waited outside while Ryan took the elevator to the top floor. He felt a little uneasy about the whole thing. Ryan has followed cases in Spanish-Harlem tenements as well as penthouses. But he also knows that the rich can be as voluble as the poor—and perhaps more so.

The apartment covered two floors. On the lower, Ryan found his way into a kitchen where a butler and maid loaded refreshments on massive silver trays. One of the cooks caught sight of him. "I know what you're here for!" she said.

"If you know," said Ryan, "then *you* tell *me*."

The cook gave him a wink. "Upstairs," she said.

On the upper floor the host, in evening dress, greeted Ryan cheerfully. "Welcome, welcome," the man said. "What can I do for you?"

Ryan stepped inside and looked around. There was an impressive number of gorgeous women per square foot of floor space. None of them, somehow, seemed married to any of the gentlemen present. In one corner of the room sat a white bull terrier, blinking his pink-rimmed eyes. At the other corner, Ryan saw a wooden crate. One of the girls, looking terrified, held a cord that would open the side of the container.

"Can I talk to you privately?" Ryan asked the host.

"Later . . ." The man waved his hand. "Now, gentlemen, you've all made your bets on the dog or the badger—"

"That's what I want to—" Ryan began.

"Pull the cord!" the host shouted to the girl. The men tensed and sat forward. "Let the dog go!"

The trembling girl gave the rope a yank, then turned and put her hands over her ears.

The side of the crate fell away. The bull terrier loped over and sniffed at the contents: a baroque, beautifully decorated porcelain pot filled with dog biscuits.

"And that, gentlemen," announced the host, "is the old badger game!"

The guests began to shout indignantly, a few of the girls screamed—possibly with relief. "If I'd known that son-of-a-gun was a practical joker," one stout gentleman muttered, "I'll be damned if I'd have put him up for the club."

Eventually, everyone decided it was funny and began to laugh. The host beamed. "What was it you wanted to see me about?" he asked Ryan.

"Nothing," said Ryan. "I just happened to be in the neighborhood."

The servants had begun to hand out drinks. The host invited Ryan to join in but the ASPCA agent politely declined. The disappointed host walked to the door with Ryan and wished him good night. The bull terrier had finished the dog biscuits and was now snoring peacefully in a corner. The dog, Ryan decided, certainly hadn't been the victim of cruel treatment. By morning, the terrier would probably be the only one in any kind of shape at all. For the others, it looked like it was going to be quite a party.

8

Chicken

Genuine badger-baiting, like all blood sports, is now illegal. Most New Yorkers prefer television, anyway. The only blood sport that has hung on to any large extent is cockfighting—"fighting chickens." Like the males of any species, roosters can be pretty disagreeable toward their rivals. But cockfighting has turned the ordinary barnyard scuffle into something else. The last thing in the world any sensible rooster wants is to get killed; but with a pair of razor-sharp steel spurs forced onto his legs, this is what usually happens. If the spectators and bettors find this amusing, the roosters would probably disagree.

Because fighting chickens carries a fine or imprisonment, the gentlemen who do it would rather avoid anybody with any inclination to uphold the law. Yet this is not always the case.

Ryan was on night duty in the shelter when the little man came in. He was stubby, tight-faced, in a neat fedora and a pinstripe suit. Under his arm he carried a brown paper parcel which he set down on a dispensary table.

"I have a problem," he said.

This hardly surprised Ryan. The little man looked as if he might have many problems. Unless Ryan missed his guess, one of the more urgent ones involved staying on the better side of the police. "Name?" Ryan asked, reaching for a note pad.

"I do not make myself clear," said the man. "The problem is not the name."

"I understand," Ryan said. "I was only thinking how much easier it would be if I didn't have to call you Hey or Mac or something."

"Frankie," the man muttered, unwrapping the parcel. He passed it over to Ryan. Inside were three defunct chickens.

"I am in the egg business," Frankie said. He went on to explain that his three prize hens had suddenly keeled over. "Just like that," he said. "One day healthy and happy, next morning gone. I want to know what's the matter with them. Outside of being dead, that is."

"Frankie," Ryan said patiently, "I want to tell you something you already know. These chickens couldn't lay an egg, not even if they wanted to lay an egg more than anything else in the world. These chickens are called roosters. You've been fighting them."

Frankie gave Ryan a look of total innocence. "I never fight a chicken in my life."

"Come on, Frankie," Ryan said. "Don't you think I know gamecocks when I see them?"

"Maybe I make a mistake about the eggs," Frankie admitted. "Now that I think about it, these chickens are always very aggressive."

Ryan threw down his pencil. "Go back to your farm. Leave the chickens here. I'll dispose of them, if that's what you want."

"No, no," Frankie protested. "Like I say, I got to find out what happens."

"What happened," Ryan said, "is they lost."

"Yeah, but they lose in a funny way. Like they get hit by lightning. I want a laboratory analysis," Frankie said. "The whole works."

Ryan nodded. He told Frankie to come back in a week and carried the parcel over to the Society's research department. Ryan already had his own ideas about the gamecocks. The report from the pathology lab confirmed it.

When Frankie appeared at the shelter again, Ryan told him the news. The roosters had been poisoned.

Frankie's face turned dark. Ryan went on: "Your friends probably grooved the spurs on the other rooster and packed in strychnine with Vaseline. The lab says there's enough strychnine in those chickens to knock out a horse. In other words, you've been suckered."

"This," Frankie said meditatively, "is the work of Big Willie. I am very disappointed in Big Willie." Frankie scowled and thought for a while. "Big Willie," he said finally, "is not following the rules of fair play."

"You mention that to him," Ryan said.

"Yes," Frankie said, "it should be pointed out firmly. I even think that Big Willie should not be allowed to fight his chickens any more."

"You might complain to the Athletic Commission," Ryan suggested.

Frankie bent forward. "Would you be interested," he said confidentially, "to know where Big Willie fights his chickens tonight?"

"I'd be real interested," Ryan said.

Frankie scribbled an address on a slip of paper and handed it to Ryan. "Here," he said. "Just go right in. You don't need to knock."

That night, the chicken fighters did not finish their program. The ones who failed to exit promptly through the windows were booked for a magistrate's hearing. Ryan did not make the acquaintance of anyone calling himself Big Willie. But he was interested to meet several others, wanted by the police for numerous reasons in addition to cockfighting.

The following week, Ryan had a telephone call from Frankie. Big Willie had not been at the last sporting event.

But if Ryan cared to drop in at another address, he might find him there.

Ryan did so. The elusive Willie was still not among those present, but the haul netted about a dozen others. Frankie called up later to apologize.

"Big Willie is evidently alarmed," he said. "He is being very cagey. This is normal, because he has a few other beefs against him. I even think he gives up personal appearances for a while. But he still has money going on the chickens. Now, you take down this number. . . ."

All in all, Frankie tipped off Ryan to twenty cockfights. At the twentieth, Frankie himself seemed a little nervous.

"This is a big one," he said tensely. "Very big. You're a nice guy. Maybe I should do you a favor and forget the address."

"You can do the chickens a favor and tell me the address," Ryan said. "Go ahead, I got a pencil."

The cockfight, according to Frankie's information, would be out of town and well up the Hudson. Ryan, like all ASPCA agents, has jurisdiction throughout New York State; so on the day of the fight, he drove north and stopped in at the chambers of the local magistrate for a search warrant.

"What's the complaint?" asked the magistrate, with a smile.

"Chicken fighting," said Ryan.

The magistrate started up angrily. "Chicken fighting? Are you out of your head? Come up here with a complaint about prostitution, numbers, dope, or something reasonable and I'll listen to you. But don't give me some idiotic charge about chicken fighting!"

Ryan repeated that he had information justifying a search warrant.

"And I tell you," the magistrate said sharply, "we don't fight chickens in this town. I haven't seen a cockfight for . . ."

Ryan looked up at the ceiling.

"Get out of here," the magistrate ordered.

"From what I hear," Ryan said, "this fight is scheduled for eleven o'clock."

"I'll be in bed long before that," the magistrate said.

"I hope so," said Ryan. "I really do."

Ryan finally got his search warrant from a Superior Court judge. That night, with two local police officers, Ryan visited the address Frankie had given him.

He visited it so quickly that a number of guests who had suddenly decided to leave were unable to do so.

The cockfight was being held in a storage room of a warehouse. Ryan and the officers smashed in the door. As soon as the spectators saw the uniforms, they lost interest in the game. Milling and thrashing around in the room, shouting at the officers and each other, they sought a variety of non-existent exits. One man tried to jump through a window— usually a satisfactory technique, only in this case there was no window. The two fighting roosters went flapping off into the warehouse. The cages holding the other gamecocks somehow got broken. The occupants flew to all corners of the room. One rooster, judging it to be morning, began to crow at the top of his voice.

Through a cloud of flying feathers, Ryan caught sight of a man in the awkward situation of trying to climb into a packing case. "OK," Ryan said, collaring him, "come out of that. You're part of the inventory."

The man straightened up, brushed a few feathers from his hand-stitched lapels. He was big and burly with a gardenia, now somewhat the worse for wear, in his buttonhole.

"What's the big idea?" he asked in a voice that had all the warmth of a plunge in the East River. "Take your hands off me. Don't you know who I am?"

Ryan gulped. "Yeah," he said. "I guess I do."

Frankie had been right when he had said the cockfight

would be a big one. At the jail, during the booking cere-
monies, Ryan had the uneasy impression that he had opened
the Social Register for the submachine-gun set. The big man
with the gardenia gave his name as Albert J. Bolsano—
which was probably correct. Only Ryan, like anyone else who
had ever read a newspaper, knew him by a much more
colorful one.

The prisoners spent a quiet night, calmer, most likely,
than Ryan's. The ASPCA agent passed several uneasy hours
in a hotel and next morning appeared in magistrate's court
for the disposition of the cases.

Mr. Albert J. Bolsano's two lawyers were already on hand,
along with Mr. Bolsano himself. They all wore fresh garde-
nias.

"You there," one of the lawyers called. "Step over here,
we'd like to talk to you.

"Now listen, Officer," the lawyer went on, "there's been a
mistake here. A very embarrassing mistake for our client."

"I realize that," Ryan said. "His mistake was fighting
those chickens."

"Chickens!" the second lawyer put in. "The whole business
is absurd. You can't make a case out of chickens. Really, I
don't think you understand the situation. . . ."

Bolsano, meantime, was looking carefully at Ryan, as if
appraising his weight and calculating the amount of cement
needed to offset it.

The lawyers took a fairly direct approach with Ryan. He
would, if he knew what was good for him, forget the whole
thing. Ryan merely pointed out that he didn't give a damn
who Albert J. Bolsano was. Cruelty to animals was against
the law. The law included chickens.

"All right," said the lawyer, "you give us two choices. We
plead guilty or not guilty. If we plead not guilty, we come to
trial, with a jury."

"Then," Ryan said, "it seems to me the problem is up to

the jury. You take your chances, just like everybody else."

"I'm not worried about the jury," said the lawyer coldly.

"Listen, Ryan," the second lawyer said. "You make us go to court with this thing. All right. As the arresting officer, you'll damned well have to be in court too."

"I expect to be," said Ryan.

"You don't understand," the lawyer went on. "I can get this case postponed from now till hell freezes over. Every damned time we go into that courtroom, I promise you I'll get a postponement. I'll have you dragging your rear end between here and New York City until you wish you'd never heard of chickens. You'll be a permanent commuter."

"Mister," Ryan said, "if I have to spend twenty-four hours a day in this town for the rest of my natural life, I'll do it. You get all the delays and postponements you want. The day this case comes to trial, I'll be sitting in that courtroom."

"You might not last that long," the lawyer said, "if you take my meaning."

"I'll worry about that," Ryan said. "But you still have another choice. Your client's guilty. Ever think about pleading that way?"

The magistrate's court opened and the prisoners, including Albert J. Bolsano, filed in. Presiding that day was a man Ryan had already met: the magistrate who had refused to give him a search warrant.

As soon as Ryan saw him on the bench, he decided that he might as well pack up and go home—and take out a life insurance policy on the way.

The judge gave no indication he had ever seen Ryan before. He shuffled his papers and went through the formalities of hearing the complaints. When Bolsano's turn came, the judge asked what plea would be entered.

One of the lawyers stood up. "Your honor," he began, "my client pleads—"

"He pleads guilty," Bolsano interrupted.

The first lawyer sputtered and the second lawyer put his head in his hands. The judge's pen stopped in mid-air.

"What did you say?" asked the judge. "I think there's some confusion here."

Bolsano got to his feet. "I said I plead guilty. This guy Ryan claims I was fighting some chickens last night. He's right. I was. That makes me guilty of chicken flicking or whatever the hell you want to call it."

The magistrate mopped his forehead. "Mr. Bolsano," he said shakily, "you understand that if you plead guilty I may have to sentence you to prison or fine you—or do both."

"You got an interesting decision to make," Bolsano said.

The judge cleared his throat. "Under the circumstances," he said, "and . . . ah . . . taking everything into consideration, I think a fine would be sufficient. The court . . . ah . . . fines you two thousand dollars." The judge rapped once with his gavel, then dropped it as if it had burned his fingers.

Bolsano reached into his pocket and peeled two bills from an enormous roll. He tossed it in front of the lawyer. "Take care of it, Jack."

On the way out, Bolsano stopped for a word with Ryan. "You know," Bolsano said, "you got guts. I really think you'd have made that rap stick. You really would have chased back and forth from New York."

"That's what I said," Ryan answered.

"You're a damn fool," Bolsano said, "but I like you. I hate to see a guy like you waste his time."

Ryan decided he would not need the life insurance policy after all.

Later, the judge called Ryan back to the bench.

"Tell me something," he said. "Last night I had the peculiar feeling you expected to run into me at that cockfight."

"Why, I never said anything like that," Ryan replied. "I don't know what gave you an idea—"

"Forget about that," said the judge. "What I want to know

is this. Suppose I had been there. What would you have done?"

"Well," Ryan began, "I locked up Bolsano—"

"But he's a crook. Everybody knows that. You mean to tell me you'd have arrested me, too?"

"I sure would," said Ryan.

Ryan drove back to Manhattan that afternoon. He carried with him one of the spectators from the cockfight: a big yellow and green parrot. Ryan could not imagine what a parrot would be doing at a cockfight, unless possibly working as referee. Since no one claimed the bird, Ryan took the parrot to the shelter, where the Society put it up for adoption.

Ryan heard no more from Frankie, except for one card, postmarked Mexico City. The climate, Frankie wrote, was wonderful, very good for his health and he hoped to stay there quite a while.

9

The Waltzing Toreadors

Bullfighting, in New York, is as much against the law as chicken fighting. So, as soon as Ryan got wind of a bullfight scheduled in Madison Square Garden he went to investigate. There he found the bullfighter, a tall, gangling young man who went under the professional name of Esteban de la Torre. Esteban was neither Spanish nor Mexican, but a local North American amateur named Wilmer. He had, so he claimed, appeared in most of the world's famous bull rings although he did not mention how long his appearances had lasted. Nevertheless, Wilmer was a great student and aficionado of the sport; to prove it, he showed Ryan his *traje de luces*, the glittering, traditional costume of the matador.

Ryan admired the embroidered jacket and breeches, agreeing that Wilmer looked very Spanish in them. However, he had to advise the dismayed matador that a bullfight is a sport forbidden by law.

"But it isn't a sport," Wilmer protested, "it's a *drama*. A great drama. Like Greek tragedy. The *corrida* isn't just a game. See it this way—man confronted with his destiny. Whether he wins, or the bull wins, it doesn't matter. . . ."

"Are you sure about that?" said Ryan.

"Ask any *torero* . . ." Wilmer began.

"Why not ask the bull?" Ryan suggested.

"You still don't understand," Wilmer went on. "Look, at the climax of the *corrida*"—Wilmer raised his hand with an imaginary sword—"there is the bull . . . there is the man. This is the moment of truth!"

"Your moment of truth is right now," said Ryan. "The truest thing I can tell you. *No* bullfight."

"But it's all arranged," Wilmer cried in despair. "What am I going to tell my *cuadrillo?* What about my *picador* . . . my *banderillero* . . ."

"Tell them the truth," Ryan said. "The show is off."

Wilmer was on the verge of tears. "Suppose . . . suppose," he said, "I don't really kill the bull? Just some fancy cape-work, a few *veronicas* and *media veronicas* . . ."

"Look," said Ryan, "I don't know what a *veronica* is. All I know is you can't work a bull with a cape. Not in New York."

"But capework isn't bullfighting," Wilmer began.

"It's bull *baiting*," Ryan said, "and that's just as illegal."

Wilmer rubbed a hand over his forehead. Then he snapped his fingers. "I have it!" he said. "I won't use a cape and I won't use a sword. I'll use a chair!" Before Ryan could protest, the bullfighter continued. "Not for the bull. For me to sit on!

"I can see it now," Wilmer went on enthusiastically, "like an etching by Goya . . . the matador sitting calmly while the bull charges. . . ."

"You mean you're just going to sit still?" Ryan asked.

"Yes!" Wilmer cried. "What an exhibition! What a triumph!"

"For you or the bull?" asked Ryan.

"I told you that doesn't matter," Wilmer said patiently. "Do you have any objections to it? Am I breaking any law?"

"No," Ryan said, shrugging, "you're welcome to sit down and let as many bulls as you want run at you. That's one of your rights as a New Yorker. But if you want my personal advice, get a soft chair. A big, padded, upholstered, overstuffed easy chair."

"The chair," Wilmer sniffed disdainfully, "will be classically simple. All wood."

The night of the bullfight, Ryan and Frank Howarth, another Society agent, were on duty at the shelter. Ryan had planned to look in on Wilmer's exhibition. The Manhattan headquarters in those days was close by the old Garden, and Ryan calculated that he had ample time. Wilmer, however, must have started his show earlier. When Frank answered the telephone, Ryan saw him listen in perplexity for a moment.

"It's the manager of the Garden," Frank said, turning quickly to Ryan. "He says there's a bull in the box seats . . . no, wait a minute . . . in the bar. Yeah," Frank nodded. "I can hear it's the bar."

"Ask him about the toreador," Ryan called, starting for the door.

"Yeah." Frank turned to the phone again. "He says," Frank advised, "what toreador?"

Ryan started up one of the Society horse ambulances and barreled over to the arena. Pushing through the crowd, he found the manager in the bar, surveying a row of broken bottles and fractured glassware. The bar itself looked as if it had been raised off the floor and set back in place—only not very well in place. It leaned at an angle that would have caused any drinker to renounce alcohol.

"The bull," said the manager, "is no longer here. He couldn't wait. He left a few minutes ago, heading down Madison Avenue." The manager pointed to a jagged hole in a partition. "He took a short cut."

"Where's the bullfighter?" Ryan asked.

"The last I saw him," the manager said, "he was about four—no, five feet in the air, traveling toward the box seats."

"He really sat on a chair and let the bull charge him?"

"Yes," said the manager wryly, "but I think he might have

changed his mind at the last minute. That was when the bull crashed into the chair. After that, he left very quickly— even faster than the audience."

The manager gestured toward the arena, where some of the spectators, venturing to return, poked among the splintered seats for their coats and hats. The breeches of the *traje de luces* shimmered from a railing.

Frank, meantime, had arrived to lend a hand. He took over the horse ambulance while Ryan raced along Madison Avenue. The calm expressions of the pedestrians gave no indication that an infuriated bull had just gone by. Even the sight of a breathless ASPCA agent clutching a lasso attracted little attention. The bull, for all Ryan could tell, had disappeared into thin air. Near Madison Square park, however, Ryan knew he was on the right track when he heard a shriek from the ladies' comfort station:

"Gladys! There's a bull in here!"

By the time Ryan quickened his pace and reached the vicinity, he felt quite sure there were no longer any ladies within a wide area. Gingerly he opened the door of the comfort station and peered in. A large black bull peered back at him.

"Mister," Ryan said, "you know you don't belong in there."

The bull snorted and pawed at the tiles. Ryan could have sworn he saw sparks flash from the bull's nostrils. He wondered, irrelevantly, where Wilmer could have gone in only half a matador costume.

Frank had backed the horse ambulance up to the ladies' room. For Ryan, now, the problem was simplified. All he needed to do was get the bull into the truck, the only distressing feature being that the bull had no intention of moving.

Ryan immediately decided against luring the bull out by any fancy capework. First, he remembered Wilmer; second, he had no cape. He did have a lasso. Ryan checked the sliding knot, gave the rope a few expert twirls and dropped the noose over the bull's horns as efficiently as any cowpuncher.

"You got him!" Frank called.

"Yeah?" Ryan shouted back. "As long as I'm on one end of this rope and that bull's on the other—I don't know who's got who."

Ryan packs a lot of strength, but no amount of tugging could move the bull. Frank added his own weight. The bull merely planted his feet more firmly and snorted at the two men.

"If this is the moment of truth," grunted the sweating Ryan, "I wish this bull would lie a little."

The only available thing stronger than the agents, Ryan realized, was the horse ambulance. He secured his end of the lasso to a concrete slab, hoping the bull would take a while to uproot it. One section of the ambulance could be turned into a sort of motor-driven ramp, or stretcher, used for hauling heavy animals into the vehicle, and Ryan saw a way to convert the mechanism into a winch. He attached his rope and started the engine.

For a time, Ryan feared that bullpower might outpull horsepower. The bull, if he came out at all, could easily take half the ladies' room with him. At last, the bull yielded slightly. His head and shoulders passed the door.

From then on, it was as easy as hauling a whale into a motorboat. The engine labored, the improvised winch screamed and the cable-reinforced lasso looked on the verge of snapping several times. Step by step, the bull drew closer to the ambulance. Finally the animal was inside, and Ryan tumbled against the doors.

Still breathing hard, Ryan and Frank drove to Madison Square Garden. Ryan reported the bull was back, safe and sound.

The manager did not appear to welcome the news. Ryan could, he explained, have the bull all for himself. He never wanted to see or hear of bulls again. As for Wilmer, he had evidently resolved to give up the sport forever. There was no sign of him in the Garden.

"But if you find him," the manager said, "you can take him along with his bull."

While Ryan pondered over the consequences of bringing a bull to the ASPCA shelter in the middle of the night, one of the Garden hands, a man named Tony, offered to buy the animal. On condition that Ryan make the delivery.

"OK," Ryan agreed. "But once that bull's on your property, he's your baby."

"Sure thing," said Tony. "What's the big deal? I don't have no trouble."

The two ASPCA agents, Tony and the bull set off for the outer edges of Brooklyn.

New York can be an exciting town, especially toward dawn and when you have a wild bull in tow. On the ferry which then crossed the East River, while Ryan had momentarily turned his back, a drunk crept into the ambulance and cheerfully climbed on top of the bull. Ryan delicately lifted him off, not wanting to see the man's evening spoiled as a result of his being squashed flat.

Tony lived on a tiny farm on the outskirts of the borough. In the moonlight, Ryan and Frank worked to bring the bull out again while Tony darted back and forth like a conspirator, warning everyone to be quiet.

"Listen, Tony," Ryan hissed, "moving a bull isn't quiet work. I can shut up, so can Frank. But I'll be damned if I know how to make the bull shut up. What's the trouble?"

Just then a bedroom window flew up. A woman in hair curlers leaned out.

"Tony, is that you?" she called.

"Yes, baby," Tony answered meekly. "We're just trying to lock up this bull—"

"A bull is it? Don't tell me you're not drunk!"

With a yell, the woman slammed down the window. A second later, she was outdoors, a buggy whip in her hand. Ryan and Frank waited patiently while she chased Tony around the yard. For her size, Ryan noticed she was remarkably quick on her feet.

"I guess that's it," Frank said, as Tony and his wife disappeared up the road.

"I guess so," Ryan nodded. "He was only a length ahead of her, but the last I saw she was moving up fast."

The two men locked the bull into an empty stall and returned to Manhattan. Tony did not show up at the Garden next day, or the next day, or the next. He did not show up at all. He had disappeared as completely as Wilmer.

About a year later, Ryan bumped into him on the street. Tony greeted him happily and pumped his hand. Ryan saw he was wearing a new suit, and a new pair of bright yellow shoes. When the ASPCA agent asked whether his wife had ever caught up to him, Tony smiled reminiscently.

"Oh, we finally get everything straightened out," he said. "For a while, she's a little nervous about the bull. But it all works out."

"What did you ever do with the bull?" Ryan asked.

"I go into the cattle-breeding business," Tony said. "I get lots nice calves, and good prices for them. Why, what else you do with a bull?"

That same week, Ryan was reminded of the bull once again, when he read a newspaper article about an American matador in Mexico City. The American had put on such an exhibition that the judges awarded him two ears. Ryan sincerely hoped it was Wilmer; yet, somehow, he doubted it.

Wilmer was not the only would-be toreador in New York. Not long afterwards, Ryan was dispatched on an urgent call to a stockyard near the river. There, on the dock, an enormous bull pawed and snorted and in general behaved like a man offering to lick anybody in the place.

Ryan leaned from the cab of the horse ambulance. "How'd he get out?" the agent called.

The dock workers neither knew nor cared. Their main interest was how—and how fast—Ryan could get the animal back where he came from. The bull, Ryan saw, was too much in the open to risk using the lasso alone. The agent could easily imagine the bull jumping off the dock and heading for New Jersey, with Ryan at the other end of the rope. However, Ryan's attention went to a number of electric cable reels. Using the ambulance as a bulldozer, Ryan shoved the reels, one by one, into position around the bull.

After that, the agent applied the same technique he had used before: rigging up a winch and hauling the bull into the vehicle. The method worked. Only the bull didn't like it. Inside the horse ambulance, he kicked and bellowed further challenges.

Ryan sped toward the stockyard. Once past the gate and in the open court in front of the office building, Ryan began looking for a place to deposit his passenger.

"Hey, you!" called a young man in an executive-looking double-breasted suit. "What are you doing with that bull?"

Ryan explained that he was trying to find a safe pen.

"That won't be necessary," said the young man. "The bull belongs to us. You can let him out right here."

"Here?" Ryan said in disbelief.

"You heard me," the man answered testily. "We're used to handling animals. He won't give us any trouble."

"Are you crazy?" Ryan asked. A few bellows sounded from the back of the truck. "Look, sonny, you go find somebody with some authority around here."

The young man drew himself up stiffly. "*I* am the authority around here," he said. "I am an officer and part owner of this company."

"Kid," said Ryan, "you may be an officer, but I don't care if you're General Grant. If you want me to let this bull loose, here and now, I'll do it. Just put your orders in writing and sign your name."

The young executive sniffed. "I'm not afraid of responsibility." On a sheet from Ryan's notebook, he jotted down his instructions to release the bull and added his name with a flourish. "There," he said. "Are you satisfied?"

"Yep," Ryan said, "and I hope you will be." He opened the ambulance. The bull shot out with all the determination and single-mindedness of a clerk at five o'clock.

"Hey," shouted the junior executive, "he's going into the offices."

"Well," Ryan reminded him, "you said he belonged here."

"But . . . but . . ." The young man sputtered and made swimming movements with his arms. "You can't let him do that . . ."

The sound of smashing glass from inside the office building suggested to Ryan that whatever the bull planned to do was already done. Running through the shattered door, Ryan found the reception desk overturned and the receptionist, shrieking at the top of her voice, perched on a filing cabinet.

Farther down the hall, two employees had taken refuge in a public telephone booth. The bull in passing had casually, and almost as an afterthought, tossed the phone booth on its side. The employees decided it was safer to stay where they were.

All along the corridor, doors slammed and terrified clerks raced up the stairs. A blizzard of correspondence, bills and other papers filled the air. With Ryan at his heels, the bull galloped the entire length of the hall and out into the courtyard again.

On the far side of the court, Ryan caught sight of a procession of cows heading for the pens. "Hey, boy!" Ryan whistled and waved his hands. The bull turned to the attack and came charging down on the ASPCA agent.

"In there!" Ryan shouted. "In there!"

The bull hesitated. He ogled the cows for a moment.

"Go on, boy," Ryan urged. "That's your fan club."

The bull decided that cows were more interesting than ASPCA agents. He joined the troop. Ryan thought he glimpsed a look of happy anticipation in his eye.

The ASPCA agent made his way back to the wreckage of the office. The young executive was nowhere in sight. The two employees had just begun to ease themselves out of the phone booth, like sailors climbing gratefully from a stoved-in boat.

Near the overthrown reception table, a stout man in shirt sleeves surveyed the wreckage. "Look at this ruin!" he cried as soon as Ryan appeared. "Nobody's going to work here for a week!"

"That's the company's problem," said Ryan.

"You're right," the man wailed. "It's my problem. I own the company! What do you want?" he went on. "Are you trying to put me out of business? Before you turn loose a bull like that, you should have your head examined!"

Ryan pulled out the sheet of paper. "I don't need my head examined, but your vice-president does."

The man read the authorization, then nodded sorrowfully. "I apologize," he said. "I should have known."

"Where'd you ever get a kid like that for a vice-president?" Ryan asked.

"Where did I get him?" cried the man. "You should only know where I got him. That no-good! He's my son," he added ruefully. "My son, the bullfighter."

10

Hospital With a Heart

If Noah's Ark had a sick bay, its patients couldn't have been much more widely, or wildly, assorted than the ones the Society treats through its medical-surgical services. At one time or another, the ASPCA hospital has been a maternity ward for a lioness; a stopping-point for flying deer; a nursery for a black leopard and her adopted litter of puppies. Admission records cover practically the whole animal alphabet and there has even been a theological cat.

Miss Agnes Riddell, Chief Hospital Clerk who took a two-week temporary job with the Society and recently retired after staying on for 37 years, recalls being briefed about the cat by the housekeeper of St. Patrick's Rectory. Until his illness, the pet spent much of the day sunning himself on the rectory steps. Passers-by would often stop to admire him, which was all right with the cat as long as they did it from a distance. When they tried to stroke him, he hissed, bushed his tail and smacked them indignantly.

He changed his behavior for one group: clergymen. If a priest wearing a Roman collar offered to pat him, the cat would beam happily, purr and roll with delight.

"They're the only ones who can touch him," said the housekeeper. "So tell the vets to be careful. I'm not saying he really knows the difference between Catholics and Protestants. I think it's the collar that does it. He'd swat the archbishop himself if he didn't have one on!"

In for treatment after losing her litter, a black leopard seemed so lonely and forlorn that Society veterinarians judged she would welcome almost any kind of young. They cautiously presented her with a litter of puppies, which she nursed and fondled lovingly. She recovered and went back to her job with an animal act before she began wondering why the little balls of fur barked instead of mewed. The lioness, also in show business, produced three rambunctious cubs during her stay in the Society's hospital. Her trainer later sold one of the cubs to Florenz Ziegfeld, who kept it in his office. The cub soon proved too spectacular even for the great Ziegfeld and the producer eventually, with much relief, presented it to the zoo.

To promote the movie *The Yearling*, Metro-Goldwyn-Mayer rounded up a herd of deer for distribution to children's zoos here and abroad. This was in pre-Animalport days and the Society offered to lodge the deer in its hospital stables until the animals found plane accommodations. The leggy, liquid-eyed deer were quiet and well behaved throughout their stay with the Society. The only hitch in the deer-lift came when one pilot made a forced landing in Britain and began unloading his cargo onto the airstrip.

The British have strict quarantine laws concerning animal immigrants and the unexpected, uncertified arrivals threw field officials into confusion. Since the deer had already landed, nothing could be done to make them un-land. The indomitable customs men collected all the disinfectant and bug spray they could lay hands on and began saturating the area, which they continued to do long after the deer had been trucked away.

The hospital's work is as varied as its patients. Recently, a blind couple appealed to the Society to help their seeing-eye dog when the animal began to lose her own sight. Society veterinarians performed an intricate eye operation to restore the dog's vision. In another case cortisone, plus heat treatment with the hospital's new diathermy equipment, helped relieve a German shepherd's arthritis.

Open-heart surgery is an extremely delicate procedure even in human hospitals; but not long ago, the ASPCA veterinarians performed the hospital's first open-heart operation. The patient, a dog, recovered completely.

ASPCA researchers are now doing some of the most exciting and promising work in the veterinary field, trying to discover ways to save animals suffering from malignant lymphoma, an incurable form of cancer.

The Society's hospital has been setting the pace for veterinary medical centers for more than fifty years. Bergh had planned an animal hospital, although he never lived to see it finished, and the hospital which the Society opened in 1912 was the humane movement's first full-scale medical-surgical institution.

The hospital kept its original location at Avenue A and 24th Street until 1950, when the Society consolidated it with the new shelter and headquarters at 92nd and York. The Society has always made it a principle—and point of pride— to have the most advanced veterinary facilities available. A major portion of the million-dollar building expense went toward outfitting the hospital, which has recently completed a new $60,000 expansion program.

The hospital treated 19,000 animals during its first full year of operation at 92nd and York. This figure has jumped 60 percent since then, and Society veterinarians now see about 31,000 patients a year.

"We hope this increase is due to improvement of the level of care," says Hospital and Clinic Director Dr. John E. Whitehead. "And," he adds, "the level of care is directly proportional to more adequately trained scientific personnel, as well as the use of new and proper equipment and drugs."

Another service which has been increasing in importance over the past few years is the hospital's handling of referrals from private veterinarians. The Society has never taken the position of competing with veterinarians in private practice and, in fact, encourages owners to take their animals to local doctors. However, as a professional courtesy to New York veterinarians, the hospital will accept patients on a referral basis. In their own offices, many private veterinarians don't have the exotic equipment the Society makes available —nuclear devices such as the hospital's new beta-ray applicator for treating certain eye cases and ulcerative conditions. Just as in any large-volume human hospital, Society veterinarians routinely perform a lot of operations which are relatively rare in private practice.

With an animal needing such specialized care, the private veterinarian is welcome to refer the case to the ASPCA hospital, and the veterinarian receives a complete report, with all supporting laboratory data, as an aid in developing his own diagnosis and continuing treatment. The ethics of human medicine apply at the Society's hospital; there is no charge to the veterinarian and, after treatment, the patients return to their own doctor.

As a further help, the Society encourages its veterinarians to publish technical articles in state and national journals, as a means of sharing knowledge with the veterinary profession.

Dr. Whitehead is a youngish, athletically built ex-Air Force man, handsome enough to have his own TV doctor show. More significantly, he has done much important clinical work in diseases of small animals and is particularly interested in radiography, pathology and diseases of the eye. A graduate of the University of Pennsylvania's School of Veterinary Medicine, Whitehead interned at the Angell Memorial Animal Hospital in Boston, then went into private practice in Hartford, Connecticut.

With a frank smile and a set of steady nerves, Whitehead usually stays unruffled, which is the way a hospital director should be; but he makes no attempt to hide his enthusiasm for the hospital's new equipment.

"This is an autotechnicon," Whitehead says, affectionately patting a big, circular device of glass and metal. "We can process a piece of tissue in twelve to fourteen hours with this. Done by hand, it would take about five days."

The autotechnicon, a memorial gift from a friend of the Society, is particularly important now, since the $60,000 expansion program centers mainly around the Pathology Department.

"We have a lot more room, and a lot more efficient working conditions, for clinical pathology," says Whitehead. "We can do blood counts, blood chemistries, urinalyses, fecal examinations, bacteriological studies—all the standard lab tests, as well as some of the more specialized ones."

The other half of the Pathology Department is devoted to histology, or tissue pathology, a means of determining the nature of the disease process by examination of tissues removed from surgical patients or deceased animals.

"This is a brand-new operation for us," Whitehead says, "and it demands some of the most intricate processes in medical research."

The Society expects the Pathology Department to be especially helpful in the cancer research the hospital does in cooperation with the famous Sloan-Kettering Institute, St. Luke's Hospital, New York Hospital at Cornell, and allied institutions.

In addition to supervising the research program, Whitehead rides herd on the program of laboratory inspections the Society inaugurated to protect animals requisitioned under the controversial Metcalf-Hatch Law.

The law requires the Society, as an institution receiving public funds, to supply unwanted animals for medical research. "Actually," says Whitehead, "the number of animals requisitioned is relatively small. The total in a year is less than one percent of all animals coming into our shelters."

Although the Metcalf-Hatch Law has ignored the question of animal welfare in experimental laboratories and made no provision for inspection, the Society's attitude is that experimental animals are entitled to protection under already existing anti-cruelty laws. No hospital or laboratory has complained about the Society's stand. Instead, they are eager to cooperate and the New York State Society for Medical Research backs the ASPCA program whole heartedly.

Whitehead strongly favors the Society's policy of laboratory inspections carried out by trained veterinarians rather than laymen. "A veterinarian is better equipped to recognize substandard conditions in animal wards," Whitehead says. Also, a veterinarian's special training lets him deal with hospital personnel on a professional basis.

Whitehead's veterinary staff checked 277,698 laboratory animals last year—dogs, cats, rabbits, rats, guinea pigs, hamsters, ducks, turkeys, pigeons, sheep, goats, horses and even some turtles. As Whitehead points out, 99 percent of these did not come from the Society. They benefit from the inspection program nevertheless and the Society has made the laboratories themselves aware of the need for first-class conditions in the animal wards.

Most of the violations Whitehead's staff turns up involve such complaints as poor ventilation, soiled cages and feeding dishes—and canine manicures, a very important detail. Unintentionally, some labs forget that a dog's nails need trimming, just as a human's. Overlong nails can be painful when the dog walks—or scratches himself, as dogs have been doing since time immemorial.

Since the inspection program, most labs have gone all out to set up clean, well-run animal wards. One Brooklyn institution, Whitehead mentions, has put in a new type of plastic dog cage with an aluminum door, and an automatic flush system that cleans the floor every two hours. Each dog also has its own self-operating drinking fountain. Many labs now have their own staff veterinarians to supervise the animals and living quarters; or call in local veterinarians as consultants.

The laboratory inspections and the research programs are carried out as additional functions of the hospital's main work: helping sick and injured animals. The hospital at 92nd and York is as busy as any metropolitan medical center for humans.

The Society's sleek ambulances, equipped with two-way radios, portable spotlights, first-aid kits and stretchers, race to about 86,000 emergency calls every year. Fractures, poisoning, suffocation, scalding—everything that can happen to a human being can usually happen to an animal, too.

To handle the accidents, as well as the thousands of cases of illnesses and ailments, the hospital follows a pattern similar to its human counterparts. It even has interns—as part of a program, started in 1960, to give young veterinarians postgraduate training. Treating over 31,000 animals a year poses a massive problem in administration, organization and treatment, and the three main departments, medicine, surgery and pathology, have now been set up as separate, but coordinated, areas of activity.

Whitehead relies on a hospital administrator, an office manager, six office workers, a foreman, and a night supervisor for the nonmedical side of the hospital. Eight attendants, lab and X-ray technicians and a night nurse fill out the medical staff which now includes 14 veterinarians.

Keeping the hospital in supplies annually demands, among other items on the shopping list, about 5,000 yards of bandages, 9,000 prescription bottles, 1,800 X-ray films. At one time, the Society had to buy meat, fish and vegetables and spend hours preparing animal food. Today, it's possible to get scientifically prepared, special-formula diets for the hospital patients—pregnant mothers, growing puppies, animals with vaccinations, intestinal complaints, kidney diseases;

even a reducing diet for overweight animals. Medicines in the hospital pharmacy are surprisingly close to those found in a human medical center: almost all of the antibiotics, serums, drugs. The hospital has also had some excellent results with the new tranquilizers, originally developed for human consumption.

In treatment, the Society's hospital has perhaps even more problems than a comparable human-oriented institution. Animals don't bore each other with details about their operations; they can't even tell the doctor where it hurts. Hospitalized animals are able to do a lot less for themselves than hospitalized humans. Even on the way to recovery, a dog, cat or other four-legged patient requires continual attention.

Each of the 14 veterinarians makes daily, 45-minute ward rounds, personally checking the progress of patients under his care. Attendants see that drinking water in the individual, temperature-controlled cages is changed three times a day. Human patients do better if they can be up and around as soon as possible and the same often holds true with animals. Dogs get their exercise, if their condition permits, every morning and afternoon in the hospital's rooftop runs. There, subsurface heating pipes keep the paving warm and free of snow.

If taking care of a hospitalized animal is a complex job, the human with a pet in hospital is, himself, usually under a strain. People worry about their pets and are anxious to know how they're doing. To make things easier on the humans, the Society sets aside two hours each afternoon between two and four, to receive telephone calls from owners and to advise them about the patients' progress. The veterinarians, too, have their own daily telephone hour, and owners may talk directly with the doctor on the case.

Famous owners are an old story to the Society. Agnes Riddell remembers reassuring one daily visitor, the late Gertrude Lawrence, about her dog's condition. Singer Jane

Froman visited the hospital every day to look in on her convalescent dog. And when the Winter Garden Theater's cat had to be admitted for treatment, his most faithful visitor was comedienne Beatrice Lillie.

The theater people all missed the cat, Miss Lillie explained. He lived backstage and spent his days among the properties, or perched on the scenery. His favorite spot was the middle of the stage itself. During performances, the cat watched the show from the wings; but as soon as the curtain came down he would stroll out again and supervise the work of the stagehands. The cat always returned to the wings before the next act began and seemed to know that the actors would not have appreciated his presence in the middle of a scene.

Everyone was delighted when the cat recovered and Miss Lillie took him back to the Winter Garden. He was probably the only theatrical cat that didn't try to hog the spotlight.

The Society's records show a yearly total of more than 43,000 days of hospitalization, but out-patients still account for the major share of the hospital's work. For a small extra fee, owners may make advance appointments and see a particular veterinarian at a specified time. Otherwise, veterinarians examine the animals in order of arrival, although emergencies always have priority.

Sometimes it's hard to tell who's having the emergency. One woman brought her cat in for minor treatment, to which the animal submitted without fuss, while the owner fainted dead away.

The hospital was also the setting for a nonmedical complication. A man and his wife took turns visiting their convalescent dog and everything was fine until the schedule got mixed up and the couple arrived at the same time one afternoon. This circumstance might ordinarily have provided cause for a happy domestic reunion. The husband, however, was escorting a female companion. The trio stepped outside to settle their differences, which must have been considerable. Next day, the wife returned to collect the dog. There was no sign of the husband. This might have been just as well. The Society is better equipped to deal with animal, rather than human, casualties.

"No animal in need of care is ever turned away" is the hospital's slogan. An owner who can't afford the regular fees pays what he can. An owner who can afford to pay nothing—pays absolutely nothing. During the Depression, charity cases reached 70 percent. In those days, when the hospital was located on 24th Street, the hospital's clients always included a good handful of urchins and waifs from the neighborhood and it was not always easy to know which needed more care: the puppy or kitten, or its ragged owner.

"What this dog should have," a veterinarian told one of the urchins who had carried in his lop-eared, long-legged pet for treatment, "is plenty of fresh meat, milk every day—"

"You're a comedian, Doc," the boy interrupted, "I don't even see that stuff at home." He stopped, and the veterinarian had the impression the boy was mentally riffling through a file of butchers who couldn't run very fast and sleepy milkmen who wouldn't notice a missing quart. "OK," said the boy, with a wink. "If that's what he needs, he'll get it."

Today, charity patients make up 40 percent of the hospital's cases, but even for the paying clients, the hospital's attitude of personal concern for its patients—a beagle with a sore paw, or an ailing ocelot—is more than money can buy.

This is why the Society likes to call it "the hospital with a heart." Purely as real estate, the hospital is impressive with its treatment rooms, half a dozen examining rooms, its two completely equipped surgical suites, its cheerful corridors, immaculate cages. But, as in all ASPCA operations, there is something more.

At the Daynemouth Ward (given and sustained by one of the Society's best friends), for example, a small box sets into the wall beside the glass door. This is the isolation area for pets suffering from contagious diseases. Inside, ultraviolet lamps, sterilizers, anti-virus and anti-bacteria sprays prevent spreading infection. Only a special staff of white-coated doctors and attendants is authorized to enter. Owners must stay outside.

But once a pet is on the mend, an attendant brings it to the glass door. The owner can see his animal. And talk to it. The small box is a two-way radio.

"Owners miss their pets as much as pets miss their owners," says Operations Director Amundsen. "With the radio, they can at least get together for a little while." He adds, with a grin, "There's nothing silly about loving an animal."

Naturally, the hospital doesn't win them all. Not long ago, a cab pulled up at the Manhattan headquarters and a young boy dashed out. His dog was ready to have puppies, he told an attendant. One of the veterinarians raced to the taxi. But the puppies had already begun to arrive and the taxi was rapidly becoming a four-wheeled maternity ward. At that point, there wasn't too much the animal obstetrician could do. The cab driver was the one who really helped the most. He turned off the meter.

11

Is This Your First Elephant?

Ryan was passing the new hospital dispensary one day when one of the younger veterinarians called him over. "I have the circus on the phone. Did you ever hear of an elephant with adenoids?" he asked nervously.

Ryan shrugged. Elephants, he supposed, could have adenoids just like anybody else.

"It's one of the animal handlers," the veterinarian said. "I can't quite make him out. It sure sounds like a case of adenoids to me. But their own vet isn't there and this guy keeps talking about a bull . . ."

"Tell him we'll be right over," Ryan said. "And incidentally, when a circus man talks about a bull, he means an elephant. In fact, he means a female elephant. That's the only kind they use."

"But I thought a bull . . ." the veterinarian began.

"In the circus," Ryan said, "a bull is still a lady."

The veterinarian grabbed his instrument case and he and Ryan drove to the circus encampment at the edge of the city. The circus was getting organized to open in Manhattan, and the grounds were littered with canvas, ropes, poles and all the confusion that only circus people understand. But even in a circus on the move it is not easy to overlook an elephant, and Ryan and the veterinarian found the elephant department quickly.

At a distance, an elephant is impressive. At close range, it can be stupendous. Nothing looms quite so large, so gray and clifflike as an elephant, especially if you aren't expecting to see one that day.

"Ryan," the vet whispered desperately, "what have you got us into?"

"This your first elephant, Doc?" Ryan whispered back.

"Well, I've *seen* them before," said the vet.

This elephant was relatively small: only about eight feet tall and weighing considerably more than Ryan, the vet and all the handlers put together.

One of the handlers formally introduced the vet to his patient.

"Something wrong with her trunk," he advised.

"What is it?" Ryan asked the handler. "You see anything inside?"

"Mister," said the animal handler, "I feed this elephant every day, I give her water, I tuck her into bed at night. But if you think I'm going to poke around a sore trunk, you got the wrong guy."

The handler had a point. Most elephants are good-natured, and even on the shy side; but a tender trunk can make them as irritable as a human with a toothache. An elephant doesn't actually eat or drink through its trunk. To drink, the elephant dips its trunk in water, breathes in and fills it up—just as a human would fill up two soda-straws without letting the contents pass his lips. Then the elephant curls the trunk into its mouth, blows out and swallows—a refreshing kind of sneeze. To eat, the elephant merely wraps the trunk around what it wants and stows the food carefully in its mouth. It can also use its trunk to spray water or to throw dust over its body, in the manner of a built-in shower-head or sandblaster. Because the elephant's neck is so short and hard to move, the trunk makes up for it, something like a mobile nose and arm combined, plus a tip as senstive as a finger. A sore trunk represents a lot of important elephant to be uncomfortable.

The veterinarian, meantime, had been walking around the pachyderm, looking at her from every angle; not unlike the man who, seeing an elephant for the first time, didn't believe it.

The veterinarian rubbed his chin. "What I think," he said hesitantly, "is that it might be easier if . . . if she could sort of lie down."

"OK," Ryan said, "you heard the doctor. Get her to lie down. Where's the bull-master?"

One of the men explained that the chief elephant handler had gone into the city. Ryan put his hands on his hips. "We can't wait for him. Come on now, let's move! Get a pair of hobbles out here. Get me a lead-chain!"

The circus men jumped into action as if the bull-master himself had unexpectedly returned. While Ryan snapped out orders and directions, the handlers attached the hardware which, on the elephant, suddenly looked fragile.

"All right, girl," Ryan soothed, "I don't guarantee you'll like this, but we're trying to help you. Down you go . . . come on, down . . ." Ryan wielded the elephant hook as expertly as any mahout. Lying down is a large-scale operation with elephants; but a few moments later, Ryan turned to the vet.

"Well, Doc, she's all yours."

The vet gave Ryan a look of amazement and gratitude. A quick examination with a cystoscope told him what he wanted to know. "It's a growth in her trunk," he said. "Not too big. But I can see how it would bother her."

"What about it, Doc?" asked one of the handlers. "You going to operate?"

"Might as well. She's not getting any better the way she is."

Treating an elephant takes team spirit. While Ryan laid out the instruments, the veterinarian anesthetized the trunk. As if trying to investigate a large and extremely delicate fire hose, the vet inserted a long, thin cutting device. In another second, the growth was out.

"I'll have this checked at the lab," the vet said. "I don't think it's malignant, but there's no sense guessing."

"And that's all there is to it?" a handler remarked, with an air of disappointment.

"That," said the vet with relief, watching the big animal climb slowly to her feet, "is about enough."

"Ryan," the vet said as they drove back to the city, "I've seen you handle cats and dogs and horses and jaguars and pandas and lizards. But you were practically running that crew back there. I didn't realize you knew anything about elephants."

"Like they say," Ryan replied, "you never asked me."

If the veterinarian had been surprised to learn that elephants popped up regularly in Ryan's career with the Society, he might have been understandably impressed by another item of information. Ryan is one of the few people—it might be safe to say the only person—to go elephant hunting in Yonkers.

Yonkers is not good elephant country; those animals, for the most part, are rarely seen in the vicinity. But it is likely that one elephant might never have left Yonkers if it hadn't been for Ryan.

The Shriners were the ones who really started the affair. The order had scheduled a convention and full-dress parade, with floats, pretty girls, a brass band, mass marching of the chapters in fezzes and regalia. Despite all this, the Shriners decided something was missing: an elephant to provide the final, perfect touch of exoticism.

Accordingly, the Shriners arranged to borrow an elephant from the Central Park Zoo. The morning of the parade, Ryan had a call from the zookeeper. The elephant was ready, the Shriners were ready; but the elephant was in Manhattan, the

Shriners were in Yonkers and it hadn't occurred to anyone, until the last minute, how to go about getting them together.

The Society obligingly offered one of its horse ambulances, and Ryan drove to Central Park where he found the zoo-keeper with an elephant hook under his arm and a worried expression on his face. Beside him stood the elephant, toying listlessly with a bale of hay.

"I don't know about this," said the zookeeper. "Rosebud's nervous today. Maybe she has stage fright or something. Or maybe she just isn't in the mood for a parade."

Ryan agreed when, two hours later, they had still not managed to coax Rosebud into the horse ambulance. Both men were drenched with perspiration; yet there is little anyone can do with an elephant who has decided not to move. The best policy, Ryan judges, is simply to maintain an optimistic attitude.

Finally, as if she had grown bored with being cajoled, leaned on, pushed and nudged, Rosebud reluctantly plodded into the horse ambulance. The ASPCA vehicle had been designed to carry some pretty large horses; but at the time of its acquisition, no one had foreseen elephants. Rosebud was only a medium-size elephant—relatively speaking, as someone might talk about a medium-sized giant—but she filled the ambulance to capacity. The keeper also packed in a howdah, a high-sided, boxlike structure about the dimensions of a small rowboat.

"What are they going to do with that?" Ryan asked.

The keeper shook his head. "Somebody's going to ride in it," he said. "It won't be me."

"Me either," said Ryan. "It probably wouldn't be legal, anyway. I'm not a Shriner."

At the Yonkers armory, the parade's starting point, the Shriners had been waiting impatiently. The band was restless, the directors of the parade had grown frazzled trying to keep all the sections in order. Ryan and the zookeeper had grown frazzled, too. On the way to the parade, Rosebud had tried several times to climb out of the ambulance. It had required all Ryan's powers of persuasion to keep her in. In the course of it, Rosebud had developed affectionate feelings toward the ASPCA agent and for the remainder of the trip had attempted playfully to reach her trunk through the wire mesh and into the driver's seat.

"You let that elephant steer this truck," the zookeeper warned, "and I get out. Here and now."

Between them, the zookeeper and Ryan attached the howdah. Ryan had to admit that, in all his experience, he had never saddled an elephant. But as far as he could see, it was the same principle as saddling a horse. So, at least, he hoped.

Three pretty girls, all in white, gauzy costumes, climbed into the howdah. Laughing excitedly, they peered down over the side like passengers on an ocean liner. One of the girls asked Ryan if elephants bit, but he assured her that was the last thing she would have to worry about.

"All right," the bandmaster called, "everybody in place." He positioned Rosebud and her cargo behind the band. Ryan and the zookeeper marched alongside.

The floats pulled into line. The Shriners formed their ranks, uniforms glittering, the girls waved happily, a whistle blew and the procession moved out. Up ahead, the band-master raised his baton and the musicians swung into the grand march.

Looking back on the afternoon, Ryan doesn't believe the bass drum did it. He exonerates the cymbals, too. The real culprit, he thinks, was a trumpet or possibly a trombone. Whichever it was, at the first blaring notes from the brass section, Rosebud raised her trunk and blared right back. Perhaps the trumpeter or trombone player had unintentionally sounded a special elephant call; if so, the message could not have been reassuring. Rosebud flapped her ears wildly, and dashed through the center of the band.

Musicians scattered in every direction. Fezzes flew through the air. The bandmaster tossed away his baton and made for the shelter of a nearby porch. The bass drum, including the drummer, rolled into the curb. The zookeeper, dropping his elephant hook, sat down in the middle of the road, totally defeated.

Ryan glimpsed Rosebud's enormous gray stern swing around a corner and out of sight, while the white sashes of her riders fluttered in the breeze. He picked up the elephant hook and hurried down the street which had, until then, enjoyed the reputation of a quiet residential area.

At the corner he saw no sign of Rosebud. Ryan settled his cap on his head. Now, in the role of a big game hunter, he strode off in the direction he hoped, logically, an excited elephant might take: straight ahead.

As he approached the intersection, Ryan detected an unmistakable spoor, a clear indication that Rosebud had passed that way. His first clue came in the form of an automobile in the middle of a newly seeded lawn. The occupants were shouting and gesticulating. Ryan believed he heard the word "elephant" mentioned several times. The street curved, but a trail of large footprints across the lawn suggested that Rosebud had not.

Ryan continued up a driveway, past the rear of one large suburban house. A picket fence lay flattened on the ground and a homeowner was studying it curiously.

Ryan hailed him. "I'm looking for an elephant."

"Yes," the man nodded slowly, "I should think you would be."

Rosebud had not decided where she was going but seemed to be acting on the policy that a straight line would bring her there most efficiently. The straight line cut through a number of back yards and clotheslines. Ryan also came upon another automobile. It was empty and undamaged. Only one thing was missing: its garage, a light wooden structure which Ryan noticed lying overturned a short distance away. In the adjoining property, he came upon Rosebud at last. She stood in the middle of a garden, pulling up geraniums. The howdah, now tilted at a jaunty angle, looked empty.

Rosebud trumpeted happily at Ryan and waved her trunk. Ryan hurried forward and looked into the howdah. He had been mistaken. The girls were still there, invisible behind the high sides. They had fainted dead away.

Shriners have a cheerful and undaunted attitude toward mishaps and they had regrouped by the time Ryan arrived with Rosebud in tow. The band had recovered its instruments and was ready to march again. The directors of the parade, seeing the girls safe once more, appeared jovial even in the face of a whole catalog of possible lawsuits.

"But we've been talking things over," said one of the directors. "We're going ahead with the parade. But this time: no elephant."

Once more, Rosebud showed no enthusiasm about climbing into the horse ambulance. Ryan and the zookeeper decided to let her have her own way.

"She likes to push things," the zookeeper said. "I don't know why. Maybe it makes her feel useful."

"If that's what she wants . . ." Ryan said. He hitched Rosebud to the tailgate. "She can push us all the way to New York."

The trip back took somewhat longer than the journey to Yonkers, but Rosebud was in no hurry. Approaching Manhattan, a thundershower moved in. Rosebud seemed to enjoy it. She trumpeted and snuffled contentedly. After the storm had passed, she amused herself by stopping every now and again to suck up water from the puddles and spray herself. In the more populous districts, she sprayed a few pedestrians.

Night had fallen by the time Ryan, the zookeeper and Rosebud reached the city. Through the winding lanes of Central Park, the moonlight glanced off the tall shape of the horse ambulance and the shadowed bulk of an elephant.

"Well, it could have been worse," Ryan said.

The zookeeper looked at him. "Worse? A runaway elephant, three fainting girls and half of Yonkers squashed flat?"

"If an elephant is going to act up," Ryan said, "it's better for it to happen with the Shriners. How would it have looked at a Republican convention?"

12

Jockeys Don't Have Pockets

Although attracting less attention than elephants, horses have not vanished from New York. The police department still maintains a mounted unit; riding academies thrive in and around the city; at fancy prices, hansom-cab horses drive sightseers through Central Park. About fifty junk dealers and hucksters have held out against mechanization and continue, with a certain amount of pride, to drive horse-drawn wagons. The ASPCA, with its two special ambulances, always keeps a horse stall ready at the hospital; and the Society's two water trucks function as mobile refreshment bars for thirsty horses during the summer.

While the number of horses residing permanently in Manhattan is limited, one activity attracts a good many pampered, fussed-over and expensive transients: racing thoroughbreds. Some people have remarked sourly that owners and racetrack stewards worry more about the horses than about the jockeys. The tracks are safer and better patrolled than most city streets. The minute a race begins, an ambulance driver starts his engine and keeps it turning over until all the entries have come in. During the race, an observer with field glasses studies each animal for signs of injury. The Society checks every track in the area and usually finds conditions excellent.

Considering the good reputation of one famous track, Ryan was surprised, early in the racing season, to learn that the Society had been receiving an unexpected quantity of complaints. Racehorses, so it was claimed, were being maltreated, lashed and generally cut to ribbons. One possible suspect, if only on the basis of his name, was a jockey called "The Ripper."

Ryan hustled out to the track. With the help of the Chief Steward, he arranged to have a few words with the Ripper in the track's private conference room.

"Listen, Ripper," Ryan began frankly, "I'm going to tell you something for your own good. Stop cutting those horses. If you don't . . ."

Despite the nickname (Ryan finally learned that a newspaper columnist had pinned it on the jockey in a moment of inspiration), the Ripper was an easygoing, goodhearted fellow. "I never cut a horse in my life," he protested. "Who needs it? If I win, I win. If I don't make it, cutting the horse doesn't do me no good."

"I don't know," Ryan said. "I've seen you out there waving that crop around. You weren't swatting flies."

"Oh, that," said the Ripper. "That's for the grandstand. I don't even touch the horse with the bat."

"Maybe so," Ryan told him. "All I have to say is this. If your horse comes in with so much as one welt on him, you'll wish you'd gone into another line of work, like crocheting doilies."

For the following week, Ryan went to the track every day. He examined the horses in the paddocks, at the starting gate, and after each race. Neither the Ripper's horse nor any other animal had a mark.

"See?" called the Ripper. "What do I tell you? A skin like a baby!"

Ryan scratched his head. The complaints had been pouring in. Yet the horses still showed no sign of being cut. At the starting gate during the last race, Ryan decided he might as well drop the whole business. If a jockey was beating a horse, he had discovered a new way of doing it. The announcer was calling the positions of the horses in the backstretch, but Ryan saw no use in waiting for the end of the race.

He began to turn away, then stopped. He suddenly knew who was whipping the horses.

Ryan found the Chief Steward. "I got my man," Ryan said. "Bring him in here."

"The Ripper?" asked the Chief Steward.

"Not the Ripper. Let me talk to your radio announcer."

The Steward called the announcer into the conference room. Ryan stood up. "Listen," he said, "I want you to repeat word for word what you were yelling into that microphone a few minutes ago."

The puzzled announcer thought for a moment. "Let's see . . . Full House was on the rail . . ."

"No, no," Ryan interrupted, "after that. You were hollering your head off up there. 'Now they're whipping those horses into the stretch! They're slashing their way home!' "

"Oh, sure," the announcer smiled. "Pretty dramatic scene."

"You know damned well," Ryan said, "not one of those jocks laid a crop on those horses."

"Well, I guess they didn't," the announcer admitted. "I just figured it sounded good on the air. You know, give the two-dollar bettors a thrill."

"Next time you give them a thrill like that," said the Chief Steward, "don't bother to come around for your last pay. I'll mail it to you."

Ryan looked up the Ripper and apologized. At the Society, the complaints stopped as suddenly as they had begun. Although some radio listeners might have wondered what had turned the slashing, whipping jockeys into such humane horsemen overnight.

Aside from overenthusiastic sports commentators, the jockeys lead a fairly tight professional life. The Jockey Club polices its own members, tries its own cases, and the penalties handed down are often more severe than any punishment the Racing Commission itself might apply. Jockeys don't have pockets in their racing silks, and while this may only be a matter of tailoring convenience, it's also a good symbol for an amazing absence of bribery. The fixed race has just about gone out with bathtub gin. Tracks are loaded with movie cameras, microphones, closed-circuit TV and Pinkerton plainclothes investigators ("The Pinks"). The horses undergo saliva tests for signs of drugs, and veterinarians run constant medical examinations.

This has not always been so. Racing has had its freewheeling aspects. At one time, the last day of the racing season at many tracks was the signal for the local residents to chain-lock their doors. "Getaway Day" around a track had all the features of a swarm of locusts. Foresighted housewives even took their laundry off the line.

Horse racing itself was less a sport than a battle of wits. Handlers and trainers seemed to take positive glee in developing new ways of wrecking the competition. But the horses, not the humans, were the ones who suffered. A single hair from a horse's tail, tightly knotted around the pastern, then concealed by a bandage, could cripple a horse in minutes. Or a pair of handlers might "broom" a horse—slapping the animal with a whisk broom, driving it back and forth between them until the horse was worn out by overexcitement. A clever operator could use a buttonhook to pull the nerve out of an ailing leg; the horse felt no pain—only, possibly, dismay when its hoof eventually fell off.

The last man in the world to be mixed up in racetrack chicanery was Ryan's good friend, Dr. Tom Childs. Dr. Tom had been among the early assistants to Henry Bergh himself. He had gone on to take his veterinary degree and had become, later, chief veterinarian for the Society. Now in his eighties, Dr. Tom had practically gone into retirement. He lived near a track in Upstate New York, and kept up a small private practice.

Ryan often visited him and could never figure out how Dr. Tom ever kept his accounts straight. Most of the neighboring farmers paid their bills on the basis of the barter system. Dr. Tom's bank balance was small. On the other hand, he had a lot of vegetables.

Ryan asked Dr. Tom if his clients had ever heard of money.

"Money?" said the old veterinarian, who had gone slightly deaf. "Yes, I'm a little short, myself. But help yourself to some beans. Very tasty. Very good for you."

Dr. Tom occasionally entered his own horses at the local track. That season he told Ryan he was convinced he had a winner. "That Blue Boy is fast. He'll run away with it," the veterinarian said glumly.

"What's the problem, then?" Ryan asked.

"The horse is fine," Dr. Tom said, "but there's one thing missing. I don't have anybody to ride him."

During Ryan's next visit, Dr. Tom appeared more cheerful. He introduced Ryan to his new jockey, a young man named Teddy. He was tall for a jockey and Ryan guessed the only reason the boy could make the weight was because he hadn't been eating too often.

"Where did you find him?" Ryan asked later.

"Find him?" asked Dr. Tom. "Why, I didn't find him. He found me."

Teddy, Dr. Tom explained, had been hanging around the track for a couple of weeks. He was there from dawn to sunset; no one had ever discovered where he lived—presuming he lived anywhere at all. Teddy had been trying unsuccessfully to find a job as an exercise boy. None of the owners seemed to clamor for his services and Teddy spent most of his days sitting on the railing, staring at the horses. He was sallow, taciturn, and his face looked older than the rest of him.

"It's a real stroke of luck." Dr. Tom beamed.

"Did he ever ride before?" Ryan asked.

"I suppose he must have," Dr. Tom said happily. "Otherwise, he wouldn't have asked to be my jockey."

"I don't like him," Ryan said. "I think you ought to find another boy."

"Nonsense," Dr. Tom said. "He'll be perfectly all right. He's staying in the house with me, I'm giving him his room and board—I can't afford to pay him anything right now. I've been watching him. He's a good boy. He's fond of vegetables, too."

Dr. Tom had bought Teddy a suit of clothes to replace the undersized jacket and oversized pants the exercise boy had been wearing. The veterinarian also had Teddy fitted in a set of racing silks and a handsome pair of boots. Even Ryan had to admit the boy looked natty in the colorful costume.

On race day, Dr. Tom gave Teddy his final instructions. The boy nodded curtly. "We'll win it," he said tightly.

"Try to get the rail," Dr. Tom went on. "If you can't, then run him easy until the first turn—"

"I say we win it," Teddy repeated. "I take this race or I bust that horse's neck."

"Good heavens," Dr. Tom cried, "don't do that! I mean, if Blue Boy wants to win, don't discourage him. But I don't want you to whip him and I certaintly don't want his neck, or any other part of him, broken!"

Blue Boy took the lead from the start. Teddy made for the rail and kept it, pounding into the turn, crouched in his saddle. Watching beside Dr. Tom, Ryan judged it no race at all, it was a walkaway. Blue Boy gained two more lengths in the stretch, and held them all the way home. Dr. Tom pummeled Ryan joyfully. "I told you!" he shouted. "He's a good boy. There's nothing like vegetables!"

The veterinarian and Ryan hurried to the paddock. Teddy, his bright silks drenched in sweat, climbed down from Blue Boy. Dr. Tom ran up to shake his hand. Teddy turned away.

"Get the Pinks," he said in a flat voice.

Dr. Tom looked at him in amazement. "What are you talking about, boy? What happened out there?"

"Nothing," said Teddy. "I win it. That's what happens."

"He's sick," Dr. Tom told Ryan. "Too much excitement."

Teddy reached into his boot and tossed a wad of hundred-dollar bills to Dr. Tom. "Keep it," he said.

"Teddy," Dr. Tom cried, "are you telling me that race was fixed? They *let* Blue Boy win?"

"You got it backwards," Teddy said. "The bookies pay me to lose."

"But you didn't lose!" Dr. Tom began.

"That's what's wrong," Teddy muttered. "I don't figure Blue Boy to start so good. I figure maybe he loses anyway. But when he takes off at the turn, and starts coming on so strong, I think I better pull him in a little. But . . . hell, Doc, I can't do that to a guy like you. So that's it. Call the Pinks."

"But my dear boy," Dr. Tom protested, "why should I turn you in? I don't want to have you arrested."

"I don't want to get arrested," Teddy said. "I just don't want to get shot. I need a couple bodyguards to put me on the train."

Two Pinkerton men escorted Teddy to the station. One of them rode with him as far as New Orleans. From there, Teddy headed west—which was the last Ryan and Dr. Tom heard.

"For his sake," Dr. Tom said, "I hope those bookies have short memories."

"I just hope," Ryan said, "they don't know much geography."

So far, no psychiatrist has specialized in horses—professionally, at least—but the trainers apply psychotherapy of their own.

Otto Bauer, a genial Bavarian and one of Ryan's acquaintances at the track, firmly believed in the psychiatric approach to racing. "Cot tamm, if a horse feels good up here," he told Ryan, tapping his forehead, "he moves good down there. That's something the handicappers don't figure. But I figure it."

He led Ryan over to a stall. "There," said Otto, "is going to be a winner. Rheingold. I make him the happiest horse on the track."

Ryan asked how he intended to accomplish this. Rheingold, as far as Ryan could see, looked more worried than happy. The horse whickered, laid its ears against its head and reared nervously in the stall. If Rheingold's position in the race depended on the horse's outlook on life, Ryan suggested that Otto would do well to bet him last.

"There is nothing wrong with him," Otto assured Ryan. "A little jumpy, maybe. What he needs is a pet. I fix him up."

Otto was only applying a bit of old horse-training lore. Ryan, ever since his boyhood, had known that highly strung thoroughbreds find it pleasant to have small animals keeping them company in the stall. For reasons best known to the horse, even the presence of a chicken has a calming influence. Perhaps race horses, by virtue of their exalted birth and status, are lonelier than cart horses; perhaps, like humans, they simply enjoy pets.

Ryan wasn't surprised at Otto's idea—but he was surprised at the pet which the horse trainer selected. Next day, when Ryan passed by Rheingold's stall he saw Otto crouched on the ground, a piece of straw in his hand, playing with a Siamese cat.

When the ASPCA inspector asked Otto why he didn't settle for an ordinary domestic shorthair, Otto shook his head.

"No, no," he said. "Only the best is good enough for Rheingold. A thoroughbred like him should have at least a pedigreed cat."

Later on, Otto lost some of his enthusiasm.

"Cot tamm," he said, "I don't think Rheingold likes cats. Not even a Siamese. Maybe they give him allergies."

However, the result was no better when Otto replaced the Siamese with a dachshund. Rheingold behaved more skittishly than ever. Otto threw up his hands in despair. "What does he want?" he cried. "Cot tamm, next thing do I get is a monkey?"

"Why don't you try a goat?" suggested Ryan.

"A goat!" Otto snapped his fingers. *"Wunderbar!* I should think of that myself. But . . . cot tamm, where do I find a goat now?"

Ryan offered to locate one but on the following day, before the agent had a chance to go goat-prospecting, Otto showed up at the track with his own animal.

"She is beautiful," Otto beamed, introducing Ryan to a shaggy, thoroughly disreputable-looking nannygoat of dubious Swiss ancestry. "My little Kaetzli! She is perfect!"

Kaetzli raised her head and made noises at Otto. She was small, even for a nannygoat, but her voice was as loud as a mule's. Otto happily bleated back at her. "You see?" he said. "We are all friends already."

Whatever Kaetzli's appearance, Ryan couldn't deny that Rheingold now seemed a better-adjusted horse. The two animals nuzzled one another and Otto nuzzled each in turn. Ryan tiptoed away from the family scene.

Kaetzli's arrival produced tangible results. The next time

Ryan stopped in at the track, Otto advised him that Rheingold's time was improving.

"Two seconds better today!" Otto said, holding up two fingers. "Cot tamm, if I know it's going to work that good, I should have bought two goats!"

Rheingold's black flanks glistened, he arched his neck proudly. Mornings, the exercise boys found him eager to prance out of his stall and begin his workout. Rheingold had a new light in his eye and every so often he would blow out his breath, curl back his lips and give a long whinny.

"He is smiling!" Otto said. "He is laughing! I never see such a happy horse."

For the week preceding the race, Rheingold did better and better. Word leaked out among the bookmakers and handicappers that Bauer's entry would be worth watching. By race day, Rheingold had become the favorite—which ruined the odds he might have brought as a long shot, but Otto was too proud to care about that.

"My Rheingold," he said fondly, "my little Kaetzli."

Ryan had promised Otto that he would come up and see Rheingold win the race. The two men stood near the track. Otto wore a Tyrolean hat with a bouquet of goat hair pinned to the crown (the hair, he assured Ryan, did not come from Kaetzli) and carried a pair of giant binoculars.

Rheingold got off to a bad start. For almost the first furlong, the other horses crowded him out. Otto began moaning desperately and clutching at his Tyrolean hat. Ryan saw Rheingold's jockey struggling for a better position.

At the turn, Rheingold looked as if he had been suddenly charged with electricity. He lunged ahead and began to move forward, picking his way through the galloping horses like a lady shopper heading for a bargain sale. Gradually he came neck and neck with the second horse, then the first. The grandstand spectators shouted. Otto tore off his hat and waved it in the air. After the turn, Rheingold took the lead in earnest. "He was only playing with them," Otto said, with relief. He passed the binoculars to Ryan.

Approaching the backstretch, Rheingold might as well have been running alone. Ryan watched him galloping effortlessly. The other entries were far behind. Through the glasses, Ryan noticed something else. The backstretch curved past the stable area; Kaetzli had been browsing nearby but at the sount of the oncoming horses, she trotted over to the rail and gave Rheingold a welcoming bleat.

Rheingold, in a cloud of dust, skidded to a dead halt. The frantic, unbelieving jockey slapped the reins, waved his arms. As the other horses bore down on him, Rheingold finally moved. But not on the track. He headed for the rail. With an easy grace, he shook off the jockey, jumped the fence and sauntered over to Kaetzli. Oblivious of the screams of the crowd and the screams of Otto, which must have reached them even at that distance, the two friends strolled back to the stables.

Later, after Otto had finally stopped crying, he and Ryan made their way to the stable yards. Ryan brushed the dust from Otto's Tyrolean hat and tried to eradicate a heel mark. It was difficult, for Otto, carried away by his emotions, had tramped very heavily on the hat.

"Look at it this way," Ryan said. "You wanted to make Rheingold feel good, and you did."

Otto nodded glumly while Rheingold nuzzled Kaetzli. "*Ja,*" he sniffed. "That much is true. Cot tamm," he added, "I hope they be very, very happy together."

Otto never raced Rheingold again. Later, he went into the horse-breeding business. Rheingold was his star performer in that activity, at least. Kaetzli stayed with her friend. Once, Otto had tried to separate them, but Rheingold got so angry that Otto had to bring back the goat immediately.

"Tell me," Otto said to Ryan. "You know all about horse racing. Why does this happen to me?"

"I don't know all about horse racing," Ryan said. "There's one thing I've never been able to figure out. How to pick a winner."

"Me too," said Otto. "But, cot tamm, I can sure pick a good goat."

13

Get Along, Little Dogies

In addition to horse racing, rodeos bring a lot of assorted livestock into New York: bucking broncos, steers, "dogies" or yearling steers, and cowboys. Ryan has met a great many of each and has discovered that some of the cowboys actually come from the Far West.

The first rodeos to visit Manhattan were, like the races, pretty freewheeling affairs. The cowpunchers applied the techniques used on the open range, in a hodgepodge of Indian wrestling and jujitsu combined with all the finesse of a saloon brawl. Calf busting and throwing the houlihan were the most common.

Calf busting begins fairly mildly. From his horse, the cowpoke ropes the calf—who usually dashes off madly in the opposite direction. But the rider then stops his horse suddenly and the calf, at the end of a tight lariat, finds himself snapped back and sailing through the air. For those who enjoy the prospect of several hundred pounds of beef rocketing skyward, this constitutes an exhilarating moment. A second later, the calf hits the ground and flattens out like a mattress. Any human in the same situation would agree that "busted" is a reasonably expressive term.

Throwing the houlihan has nothing to do with Irishmen. Perhaps an Irishman first invented it, although even an Irishman might find it a little rough. In the houlihan, a steer wrestler manages to seize the horns of the running animal,

149

twist its neck and jam the horns into the ground. Undeniably, throwing the houlihan takes considerable muscle and determination. But the cowboy has the principle of the lever and the law of gravity working for him. With horns planted firmly in the earth as a pivot point, the steer performs a reluctant somersault, arcs end-over-end and crashes to the tanbark. The maneuver can result in a twisted spine or a broken neck—not for the cowboy, but the steer.

Some cowboys also prefer to ride with locked rowels. As long as the rowel, or wheel of the spur, can spin freely it can goad the horse but not actually cut him. A rowel taped down or locked stationary by an added cotter pin can slice like a razor. The horse, understandably, moves a little faster.

The ASPCA exercises no control over what happens at rodeos outside of New York; but within state boundaries, locked rowels, busting and the houlihan are forbidden. Stock owners and the cowboys themselves have been glad to cooperate, although ruling out these methods makes the sport more of a sport and less a foregone conclusion. The Society hasn't had over a dozen provable complaints in as many years.

The ASPCA, however, continues to inspect all rodeos. Reading the advance publicity for a big rodeo opening in Madison Square Garden, Ryan noticed something that made him feel uneasy even before the show started. Putting the notice in his pocket, he drove to the garden and looked up the rodeo manager.

"Is it true," Ryan asked, "you got wild horses in this show?"

The manager, a New Jersey man named Oklahoma Dutch, said that it was. "If I advertise wild horses," he added, "this crowd's going to see wild horses."

"You want to ruin your show?" Ryan asked. "You know damned well a wild horse won't buck. All he'll do is plant his legs and stand there."

"All I got is wild horses," Oklahoma Dutch said. "Besides, it sounds good in the advertisements."

"It may sound good," Ryan said, "but you're going to look pretty silly with a bunch of horses on a sit-down strike. Why don't you rent some real bucking broncos?"

"These horses will buck," Oklahoma Dutch said, "when the time comes. It's guaranteed."

"That's what bothers me," Ryan said. "You wouldn't think of using a hot-shot on them?"

"Who needs a hot-shot?" Oklahoma Dutch said innocently.

"You," Ryan answered. "But you better not use one."

Ryan left the Garden. Unless Oklahoma Dutch had figured out a way to turn a wild horse into a bucking bronco by hypnotism, Ryan was sure that, in spite of everything, the cowboy would have to rely on a hot-shot. This battery-operated contraption was designed to jump a spark between two strips of copper. Oklahoma Dutch was right to this extent: if his handlers burned the horses with the device, the animals would, indeed, be guaranteed to buck. A hot-shot could be guaranteed to make a wooden Indian jump—and very actively.

On the opening night of the rodeo, Ryan and another Society inspector were in the audience. As Oklahoma Dutch had predicted, the wild horses outbucked anything on four legs. Sitting above the pens, Ryan saw what he had expected to see. Just before each horse burst loose, two handlers busily applied the hot-shot.

Ryan climbed down from his seat. "Those sparks aren't skyrockets," he told the surprised handlers.

Since Ryan was in civilian clothes, the two cowboys at first took him for an interested bystander; until they found themselves arrested, along with Oklahoma Dutch.

Arraigned for cruelty, Oklahoma Dutch and his men appeared in court with their lawyer, a short, stout man with a string tie and a Western accent he might have developed for the occasion.

Ryan had confiscated the hot-shot and presented it in evidence, The lawyer chose to disregard the gadget. Instead, he concentrated on the great traditions that had built the West. He evoked covered wagons, the Pony Express, Grand Canyon and Yellowstone National Park. He delivered a most eloquent speech, painting the cowboy as the inheritor of this glorious past—but Ryan could not grasp the connection between a glorious past and burning horses by electricity.

"Your honor," Ryan said, "this hot-shot is damned painful and that's all there is to say about it."

"On the contrary, your honor," the lawyer protested. "This instrument is a perfectly legitimate aid to—ah— stimulating the natural propensities of these animals—"

"The hell it is," Ryan muttered. "It burns the bejesus out of them."

"It has a mild, almost beneficial effect," the lawyer went on. "Many of the animals even seem to enjoy it. I have heard that some go so far as to indicate a desire to have it applied more frequently."

"That's something I'd like to see," Ryan muttered again. The judge, Ryan guessed, was not a horseman; indeed he seemed impressed by the lawyer's presentation.

"This device," the lawyer concluded, "does not injure horses. Since it does not injure horses, my clients therefore cannot be guilty of perpetrating any kind of cruelty. . . ."

Ryan decided there was only one way to settle the matter. "Your honor," he said, "I request your permission to demonstrate this hot-shot."

The judge blinked. "Well, really . . . I don't see that the court can allow a horse to be brought in . . ."

"I wouldn't use it on a horse," Ryan said. "But I'd like to use it on the defendants' lawyer."

"This is ridiculous," the lawyer sputtered. "It's against the dignity . . ."

"Well, what about one of your clients?" Ryan said. He glanced toward Oklahoma Dutch.

The lawyer conferred hastily with the three cowboys. "Your honor," said the lawyer, after a few moments, "any one of my clients would welcome the opportunity to have this instrument demonstrated on his person. But I regret to advise the court that these men are suffering from a dangerous heart condition. Even the slightest shock . . ."

"What, all three of them?" the judge asked.

The lawyer nodded regretfully.

"I don't want anybody to think," Ryan said, "that I'm doubting anybody's word. But what do you say we run over to Bellevue and get a cardiogram on these men—just as a matter of record."

Once more, the lawyer conferred with Oklahoma Dutch and submitted that adjourning to Bellevue for a cardiogram would not be in the best interests of his clients.

Ryan suggested calling in any cowboy from the rodeo, since it was unlikely that all of the cowpunchers would have heart conditions. The lawyer objected to this as immaterial and irrelevant.

"That doesn't leave us much to choose from," Ryan said. "I'm willing to put that hot-shot on myself."

The lawyer objected again. Ryan's reactions to the device, he argued, could not be considered unbiased and impartial.

"How about you, Judge?" Ryan asked.

"Me!" gasped the judge. "If you think I'm going to let . . ." He stopped and considered for a minute. "Officer," he continued, "if you can present a fair demonstration of this device—without using anyone present in this court as a guinea pig . . ."

Ryan remembered he still had Oklahoma Dutch's advertisement in his pocket. "Your honor," he said, "I think I can show you exactly what I mean."

He approached the bench and unfolded the sheet of paper. Ryan hooked up the copper strips to the batteries. The hot-shot was now operational.

Holding the sheet in one hand, Ryan applied the spark. A burned and smoking hole appeared immediately. He moved the hot-shot to another portion of the sheet. The scent of smoldering paper filled the courtroom.

"My God," said the judge, rapping his gavel angrily, "do they really use that on horses?" He found Oklahoma Dutch guilty as charged. "I'm not going to lock you up," the judge said. "I'm only going to fine you. This time. But I warn you, if I ever hear another complaint about you—I don't care what it is—I'm going to be very strongly tempted to let this officer demonstrate that hot-shot on you!"

Later, Oklahoma Dutch telephoned Ryan. "Listen," he said, "I want to talk something over with you. Why don't you stop over at my hotel. . . ."

Ryan declined the invitation. Even though Oklahoma Dutch came from New Jersey, Ryan feared that the rodeo manager might have acquired some Western ideas about revenge. A fast draw was not one of Ryan's accomplishments and he had never considered himself top gun in Manhattan.

"I'll talk with you, Dutch," he said. "In the middle of Madison Square Garden. And if you don't mind, I'll bring a couple of friends."

The cowboy agreed. Later that afternoon, Ryan found the manager in the arena. Oklahoma Dutch, to Ryan's surprise, appeared mild and subdued.

"All right," said the cowboy. "I been thinking over this whole business. You're too good a lawyer. I don't want any more trouble and I'll be damned if I'll take a chance. That judge might just keep his word and use that hot-shot on me.

So let's talk. I want a clean show and a good show. What do you want me to do?"

Ryan, after recovering from the shock of Oklahoma Dutch's new attitude, proposed a few ground rules.

"No busting," Ryan said, "no houlihan. No locked rowels."

Oklahoma Dutch nodded reluctantly.

"Tell your boys to quit biting those steers, too," Ryan went on. "No eye gouging. No tail pulling. And tell them to keep their fingers out of their noses. The steers' noses, that is," Ryan added. "I don't care what they do with their own."

"Oh, something else," Ryan continued. "They should get rid of the strings up their sleeves."

"Strings?" Oklahoma Dutch asked.

"Come on, Dutch," Ryan said, "You know what I mean. The strings with chloroform pads on the end. If your boys can't handle a steer when he's wide awake, you better send them back to the ranch."

"OK, OK," the manager sighed, "no chloroform." He shook his head in grudging admiration. "Ryan," he said, "I can't figure it. You know more tricks than I do. How'd you learn?"

"Easy," Ryan said. "A horse told me."

14

Orphans

For most of his life, Ryan has been helping horses and other animals out of trouble. But humans get into as many difficulties as their pets. While they don't necessarily climb trees or jump into chimneys, New Yorkers, like people everywhere, are subject to the normal human frailties. They fall sick, die, have nervous breakdowns, pick fights with opponents bigger than themselves; they have accidents and wind up in hospitals; sometimes they even wind up on the shady side of the law.

If owners are responsible for their pets, pets can't always be responsible for their owners. Through no fault of its own, an animal may suddenly find itself a temporary, or permanent, orphan. In addition to rescue work strictly speaking, the Society devotes one whole branch of its operations to this type of case. In a single year, the Society's Medical Stray Ward cares for as many as 2,600 animal orphans.

Set up more than twenty-five years ago, the Medical Stray Ward functions as a service for sick or injured creatures without homes. The Society always believed that a suffering animal was entitled to medical treatment whether it had an owner or not. The Medical Stray Ward put this principle on a highly organized and extensive basis. Today, if there is a chance of easing pain or saving an injured stray's life, the Society's veterinarians work to do so.

Francis Melvin, recently retired District Manager of the

Manhattan Shelter, has been involved with the Medical Stray service ever since it began. Owning an accent as Scottish as a haggis and as warm as a plaid, Melvin has carried bleeding, broken animals into the operating rooms, sat up with them, done extra duty as a day-and-night nurse. Like Ryan and all the Society's front-line staff, Melvin is a skilled animal handler. In the days when the Society had to manage with a severely limited number of veterinarians, Melvin himself helped out with some of the treatments.

The Medical Stray Ward, like the other ASPCA services, has grown to include much more than originally planned. Animals orphaned for any reason now find a foster home with the Society until adopted—or until their owners disentangle themselves from their personal problems and reclaim their pets. In Manhattan, a number of these problems make headlines. Animal guests of the Medical Stray Ward have belonged to some highly publicized New Yorkers, have figured in lawsuits, divorce cases and all the bizarre varieties of urban wrangling. A Pekingese even helped crack one of the city's notorious murder cases.

The little dog had been brought to the Society's shelter after the brutal killing of its two owners, a girl and her mother. For a time, the Pekingese represented about the only clue city detectives had to go on, and they spent a good part of their time finding out more about the dog.

What, they wanted to know, was the dog like? Was he a shy, retiring sort? Friendly or unfriendly? Did he bark much?

Melvin advised the detectives that the little Pekingese had a loud voice and didn't hesitate to use it. The dog was nervous, jumpy, leery of strangers. This scrap of information turned out to be a crux of the investigation. From all the evidence, the dog hadn't barked once during the night of the murder. Melvin agreed that a stranger would have set the Pekingese barking at the top of its lungs, and the police explored the possibility that the dog knew the killer of the two women. And so it was. A boarder, on friendly terms with the animal, had committed the crime.

Not all the Society's medical strays reach such a degree of publicity. For many of the city's anonymous millions, New York can be a lonely, unhappy town and their animals suffer in consequence.

Dear Doggie, a woman wrote to her pet chow, *for three days I have waited for some kind of word from you. . . .*

Too emotionally disturbed to realize that animals can't read, the woman finished her note, propped it on a table and swallowed a massive dose of sleeping pills.

A rescue squad found her barely alive and rushed her to the hospital. The dog waited patiently at the Society's shelter throughout its owner's long and difficult period of therapy. In time, she returned to claim her pet. She had learned something often easy to overlook: that an animal's love, like a human's, no matter how strong it may be in reality, truly exists only when we recognize it.

There would seem to be no end to the circumstances bringing animals to the Medical Stray Ward. One harassed hotel clerk, who sounded on the verge of nervous collapse, called the Society to help him decide whether he was seeing things.

"I have a woman here," he said, "registered a couple weeks ago with a Scotty. Now, we don't usually allow animals, but she was so pleasant, and the dog seemed like a good little fellow . . . well, you can't go by the rules all the time.

"Everything went fine," he went on. "She'd take the dog out for his walk once or twice a day. But then . . . but then . . ." The clerk hesitated. "I can't quite explain this. After a while, I'd see her come *in*. But I never saw her go *out*. She always had the Scotty with her on a leash. But I swear, every so often that dog looks different to me. I don't know exactly how . . . maybe a tiny bit heavier, or darker, or *something*. . . .

"Do you know anything about Scotties?" the hotel clerk pleaded. "You've got to help me get a grip on myself. She isn't here now. I'm going up to the room. Could somebody from the Society come around? If I find what I think I'm going to find, I'll need you. If I don't, you can call Bellevue— and let them come and get me."

The Society dispatched two agents. With the hotel clerk, they saw the answer to the mystery. The woman didn't have a single Scotty. She had dozens of them, all practically identical. Scotties romped through the bedroom, the living room, emerged from closets, wagged their tails from the tops of dressers, gleefully chewed on the rugs and valiantly pulled the stuffing from the furniture. If they barked, it must have gone unnoticed; or else the Scotties were smart enough to keep their mouths closed. The ASPCA counted thirty dogs.

By the time his guest returned, the clerk had reached the limits of his patience. One Scotty was fine; thirty had pushed it too far. The woman would have to leave. "Tell me one thing," the clerk asked as she assembled her animals. "Where are you getting them?"

"From another hotel," she said; then added huffily, "They don't like dogs there, either."

The Scotties filled up a good section of the Medical Stray Ward until their owner found another place to live. She reclaimed the dogs, but not a word did she say about her new address. Melvin often wonders to this day whether an unsuspecting hotelkeeper somewhere in New York is lodging thirty Scotch terriers.

Medical strays arrive at the Society from far beyond New York. The freight manager of one of the railroads telephoned Melvin to report that yard employees had found a dog in a lumber car.

"He's breathing," said the manager, "but that's about all. I looked up the records on the car. It's from the Northwest. The dog must have been locked up for two weeks at least!"

The Society rushed an ambulance to the freight yard. The dog was in worse condition than expected. Starved, almost completely dehydrated, the unconscious animal could barely gasp. On emergency alert, the ASPCA veterinarians began working the moment the dog arrived. For most of a day and night the animal wavered between life and death. The veterinarians continued intravenous feeding and all the supportive treatment they knew. The dog rallied, took a slight turn for the better. Meantime, he had become famous.

Reporters always keep an eye on the Society. Like police court, the fire department and the United Nations, the ASPCA is a sensitive spot for newsbreaks. Within a day, practically every paper in the city carried a story about the dog. Journalists kept almost as close a watch as the Society over the animal's progress.

The dog was definitely on the mend for a time; then, gradually, he turned listless. From a medical viewpoint, the veterinarians could find nothing wrong. Melvin, like any knowledgeable dog owner, guessed the trouble. The animal was grieving for his owner.

Melvin and the Society's Director of Operations, Arthur Amundsen, talked the situation over. They could easily find a new owner for the dog, but neither man believed that would do the trick. The dog wanted his own master. The Society appealed to the railroad, the newspapers, to anyone who would help with the impossible job of identifying a stray animal from a pile of anonymous lumber. A lumbering trade association took a hand; after days of checking, tracking and backtracking, the organization came up with the first tangible lead. They pinpointed the station from which the car had originated, and wired a local man to inquire about any lost animals.

Finally, the Society had its answer. The dog belonged to a thirteen-year-old boy, the son of a sheriff in one of the remote lumbering regions. Since the boy couldn't be there in person, the Society asked for the next best thing: a piece of clothing the dog might recognize.

Promptly, an airmail package arrived. It held a well-worn undershirt.

The undershirt of a thirteen-year-old boy is an unmistakable item in its own right. For the dog, it was absolutely unique. He sniffed, rolled on top of it, yelped excitedly and wagged his tail for the first time since his recovery.

Even better news followed. At its own expense, the trade association was flying the boy to New York.

At La Guardia Field, news photographers jammed the area of the plane's arrival. The ASPCA sent an ambulance with the dog; and it was Francis Melvin, beaming all over his Scots face, who held the dog in his arms as the plane door opened and the young owner stepped down the ramp.

If the boy and dog expected to go home on the return flight, they were mistaken. The city had taken a fancy to the reunited pair, and for the next ten days the boy and his dog were photographed, interviewed, talked at and talked about. Finally they flew home again, happy and exhausted. Ten days of publicity in Manhattan can be, in some respects, more trying than fourteen days in a boxcar.

A boy recovering his lost dog always makes a heartwarming story. But the Society offers help to any animal that needs it. In its own operations, the Medical Stray Ward can match the variety of animals cared for in all the ASPCA shelters. This section has looked after kinkajous, ocelots, jaguars, lions, a broken-winged eagle rescued from an ice floe—and one of the rarest animals, a pure albino ferret discovered in one of the most ordinary of environments, a local cigar store.

The Society welcomes all animals, although there must

surely be times when this principle is sorely tried. One of the express companies had asked the Society to take charge of an abandoned shipment of live cargo, and the ASPCA agent who answered the call found a number of burlap sacks waiting for him.

"What's in them?" he asked.

"Snakes," answered the expressman laconically.

"What kind?"

"Mister," said the expressman, "do you think I'm fool enough to open those bags and find out?"

In the Manhattan shelter, the Society workers discovered the bags to contain several dozen large snakes. The reptiles were brownish-yellowish, hooded, with a curious spectacle-shaped insignia.

"Mon!" cried Melvin. "Those beasties are cobras!"

To anyone else, even the most confirmed animal lover, a brigade of venomous serpents might have been a shade less than welcome. Not so to the Society. Melvin and his men rounded up all the tanks and aquariums they could find, decanted the cobras into them, put weighted screening on top and locked the guests in an empty room.

After the cobras had been comfortably bedded down, to their own satisfaction and to the great relief of their custodians in the shelter, Melvin called the zoo.

Next day, the zoo truck gratefully collected this unexpected gift. Later, Melvin got to worrying. There had been a number of dead cobras, sorted out and disposed of; no one had counted exactly how many live ones remained. The ASPCA men had checked the room for stragglers, but Melvin still felt uneasy.

To ease his own nerves more than anything else, he went down the hall to the cobras' former quarters and looked in. Standing there a few moments, he saw nothing. As he turned to go, a sleepy-looking cobra stretched out its length and peered at him from the corner.

An empty fish tank still stood in the room. Melvin turned the aquarium on its side and tiptoed out, locking the door behind him. He returned with a broom in his hand and half a dozen men at his back. Very cautiously he bent down and gently nudged the cobra into the tank. One of his helpers ran forward, righted the aquarium and slapped a screen over it.

"Laddie," said Melvin, "gae call the zoo and ask: have they room for ain mair?"

The Society has learned not only to take snakes in its stride, but to live with them on the most cheerful of terms. The number of resident serpents varies. One day, the staff may be practically up to their ankles in reptiles; the next, the shelter may seem empty without them. Sometimes, however, one snake can make up a crowd.

Such was the case with a gigantic boa constrictor, a fugitive from a lady snake charmer in Coney Island. The boa had disappeared in midsummer and the police, at the time, had cordoned off the entire area. The snake hunt yielded no results—except some for speculation as to exactly how such a big reptile could lose himself so thoroughly. A boa constrictor in busy Coney Island should not present the same problem as a needle in a haystack.

This one did. The boa showed no sign of its whereabouts until the following November, when two workmen started repairing an old garage. One of them, perched on a stepladder to install a light bulb, found something more electrifying. The front part of the boa coiled comfortably about the light fixture; the rest of it seemed to stretch all around the garage roof. ASPCA agents, working with the police emergency squad, disentangled the boa from the rafters and put it in the biggest thing they could find: a long glass showcase.

A patrol wagon lugged the installation to the Manhattan shelter, where it stayed for the next ten days. The big showcase took up so much room that visitors, without looking at the contents, might have wondered whether the Society was now importing Egyptian obelisks or opening a department store. The snake, which preferred its home in the garage, also had the habit of lunging irritably at passers-by. Some people felt uneasily that if the powerful boa kept on with this, it might wear a hole through the glass.

Melvin finally located the snake charmer and conveyed the good news. She could have the snake any time she wanted.

"Forget it," said the snake charmer. "You can have him. I'm working with a python now."

As he reached for the phone to call the zoo, Melvin breathed a silent prayer that this time the snake charmer could manage to keep her act together.

The Society has provided room and board for most of the common and uncommon species of reptiles in the United States. It has also cared for snakes found freeloading in banana shipments from South America. The Society people are pretty good at identifying their charges—but try to avoid overconfidence. Melvin in particular remembers one visitor, a variety he had never seen before. Ordinarily, he would have handled it with his usual nonchalance; this time, out of curiosity, he checked with the late Dr. Raymond L. Ditmars, the famous herpetologist, at the zoo.

"Aye, he's a hondsome one," said Melvin. "A nice red wi' a bit o' yellow—"

"Red and yellow, you say?" asked Dr. Ditmars. "Would he have black bands, too?"

"He does indeed," answered Melvin.

"Do me a favor," Dr. Ditmars said. "If he bites you, be sure to let us know."

Melvin's colorful guest was a coral snake, one of the most deadly in the world. The Society now makes a practice of checking all its reptile visitors with the zoo.

Snakes, for the most part, quietly mind their own business, content to stay in their tanks without fuss. From a handling viewpoint, some of the birds of prey—the hawks, falcons and eagles—give the Society a tougher time. A woman reported an injured vulture in her back yard, the Society captured the bird, treated it and put it in a cage to recover.

The vulture enjoyed a rapid convalescence and developed an eager appetite. Melvin himself often took charge of feeding the bird, although he never dared go near the vulture without first donning a pair of heavy gloves. The vulture did not have the world's sweetest disposition, and the possibility of a few ASPCA fingers in its diet appeared not to concern it. For all his skill in handling animals, Melvin always approached the bird with extreme caution.

Meantime, the vulture continued to eat the Society practically out of house and home—while the Society wistfully hoped that someone would show up to claim it. Within a week, someone did. A towheaded boy of no more than ten stepped up to Melvin's desk one afternoon.

"Somebody says you people found a big bird," he said. "I think he's mine. Can I go see?"

"Laddie," Melvin told him, "the only bird we have here now is a great strappin' vulture, squawking like a door hinge and eatin' like a horse."

The boy nodded. "That sounds like him. Thanks for looking after him. I'll take him home now."

"Och, laddie, laddie!" Melvin cried. "The beastie will take your hand off. That's not a pet for a bairn!"

The boy insisted. Melvin finally led him back to the vulture's cage.

"I knew it was mine!" the boy shouted joyfully.

The vulture looked up. The boy walked over to the cage. Like a cat waiting to have its ears rubbed, the vulture cocked his head against the mesh. The boy tickled the bird's neck. Had it been possible, the vulture would have purred.

Melvin watched in amazement. "Laddie," he asked, "where did ye ever learn to handle a bird like that?"

"I don't know," the boy said. "I guess I'm just used to them. I got another one at home."

The size of a pet-owner's bank account does not concern the Society. Neither do the pet-owner's morals. Some years ago, in the heyday of Manhattan's after-hours amusements, the city police were constantly rounding up contingents of ladies of the evening. The Society always looked after their pets until the girls, eventually emerging from the lockup, came around and took them home again.

Since most of the girls immediately launched into their old profession, and the police force kept hauling them in with the same persistence, a good many of the dogs, cats, canaries and fish repeatedly turned up in the Medical Stray Ward.

The Society people came to know these animals well, and it was not unlike a happy homecoming when they appeared. One day, in addition to all the regulars, a large parrot arrived—temporarily homeless as the result of a raid on the apartment of a certain Miss Bubbles La Mar.

Miss La Mar had received a fairly short sentence and the Society prepared to house the parrot until its owner's release. Later, however, Miss La Mar sent word to the Society that she was getting out on good behavior and going back to Ohio. The Society was welcome to the parrot.

"We sure won't have any trouble finding a home for that bird," one of Melvin's assistants remarked. "He's a beauty."

Melvin nodded. "Aye," he said, "there'll be many wantin' to adopt him. But mind! Don't let him go to any home where they have wee ones."

"No children?" asked the puzzled assistant. "But he'd make a wonderful pet for a kid. . . ."

Melvin shook his head. "Adults only."

"Why? Does he bite?"

"No," Melvin said. "He talks. So if the bairns are after learnin' the facts of life, they'd best be askin' their parents —not a parrot!"

15

23,000 Cinderellas

"What we want is a puppy," the man said, "an ordinary puppy. But he's got to be ordinary in a special way."

The visitor to the Manhattan Shelter's Adoption Ward spoke on behalf of a young Italian couple standing quietly and patiently near the door. The woman twisted and re-twisted her handkerchief. The man occasionally raised his head and bent forward, trying to guess the course of the conversation.

Thus the ASPCA Adoption Service began an extraordinary dog-hunt for a dog that wasn't ordinary at all. To a small boy named Nunzio D'Ambrosio, it was the most special animal in the entire universe. It could never really be found because it was dead.

The D'Ambrosios had brought their five-year-old son and his pet to the United States. Sailing into New York harbor, Nunzio thrilled to the Statue of Liberty and the skyscrapers. He knew exactly where the Empire State Building stood and how it looked against the clouds. His parents told him all about it, and about the shape of the skyline, the other ships in port, the colors of the automobiles. They had to. Nunzio was blind.

The D'Ambrosios had made the trip for one purpose: to find out from a prominent eye surgeon whether Nunzio would ever see again. After weeks of examinations, they received their answer. The only pictures Nunzio would ever have—of his parents, his puppy, the Statue of Liberty, a Manhattan taxicab or the fountains of Rome—would have to reach him through his fingertips, through sound, scent, but never sight.

Nunzio's parents sadly prepared for the return voyage. But, during one period when Nunzio was in the hospital, the puppy sickened and died.

Nunzio knew nothing of this; nor did he know he was going to be blind for the rest of his life. He would find out about his eyes soon enough. No one could spare him that. The loss of the puppy was something else. Doctors couldn't restore Nunzio's sight. Now his parents only wanted to know: could the Society restore one small puppy?

It's easy to find an ordinary dog. But not one exactly like another. Mixed breeds (using the polite term) don't come in carbon copies. Nunzio's puppy had had a special slope to his rear end, his tail had curved in its own utterly impossible way. There had been a certain flop to his ears, a certain feel to his coat.

The Society had plenty of puppies like that. Almost. Not quite.

A call went to all ASPCA shelters for the kind of dog no one would look at twice—unless you happened to be completely in love with him. Society workers had a detailed description of the most-wanted puppy in New York.

Had the D'Ambrosios wanted a trained seal or a zebra, the search would have been simpler.

The Society was still searching on the eve of the D'Ambrosios' scheduled return. Mrs. D'Ambrosio had even taken Nunzio to the ship, to get him settled and comfortable before the voyage.

One of the shelters telephoned. Of the hundreds of puppies that ASPCA workers had examined, this was the perfect replacement. Maybe. There is an undefinable difference between the specifications of a puppy and the puppy himself.

Mr. D'Ambrosio dropped everything and went to see the little dog. In size, shape, weight, even in the texture of the coat, the puppy was identical to Nunzio's pet. Only a couple of markings varied slightly. Nunzio, unfortunately, would never see that.

On the deck of the ship, the little dog ran to the arms of a master he had not seen until that moment. For Nunzio, who had never seen the dog and never would, the puppy had always been there.

Everyone admits this was, technically, a deception. As a deception, it was also one of the gentlest swindles ever perpetrated. The genuine thing was love; which makes up for anything else. Who, after all, worries about technicalities? Not small boys. Certainly not small puppies.

Nunzio D'Ambrosio's beloved impostor was one of some 23,000 dogs, cats and other animals who, each year, win the biggest prize of their lives: a home. Ryan spends his time rescuing animals; the Society's Adoption Service takes it from there.

The ASPCA adoption wards are a combination show window for people looking for a pet, and a wistful waiting room for dogs and cats who want nothing more than to be wanted. The number of adoptions amounts to something like 10 per cent of the animals handled through ASPCA shelters. This low figure is not as low as it seems. Most of the animals entering the shelter are incurably sick or hurt beyond recovery; the Society painlessly puts them to sleep. The majority, in fact, are put to sleep at the owner's request. If it has any choice at all, the Society always offers an unwanted animal for adoption.

As June Eliot says, "We'd rather find them a home than a heaven."

For a homeless animal, the two words are synonymous.

Prospective owners of puppies, kittens, mynah birds, parrots or other animals may adopt pets from any of the Society's shelters in New York City and beyond. This shelter system is the framework for all ASPCA operations.

In addition to being a reception and adoption center for animals in Manhattan, the four-floor shelter at 92nd and York includes the new hospital and administrative offices. The 30-year-old Brooklyn shelter handles more animals than any other in the country—about 49,000 per year. With this kind of volume, Brooklyn has had its share of boa constrictors, lions and ocelots. One night, a Brooklyn agent answered a call about a bear on the loose. For some reason, he got the impression it was a small honey bear, or kinkajou—which is not a bear at all. Instead, he found a full-grown grizzly, about as far from a honey bear as anything could be. He captured it, with the help of a police squad. The owner, an absent-minded trainer who had somehow lost track of the animal, finally turned up to claim it.

Newest ASPCA shelter is in the Bronx, a $350,000 facility built in 1956. Five times bigger than the shelter it replaced, its glass-fronted adoption kennels make sparkling showcases for available animals. Piped-in music soothes the four-legged guests and probably does quite a bit for the busy humans, too. Each outdoor dog-run contains the ultimate detail: a bright red fireplug.

In Queens, the adoption ward is a century-old farmhouse. Three other big, rambling buildings house kennels, license office and garage. The ivy-draped Richmond shelter dates from 1935 and serves the Staten Island area.

Outside New York City, the Society runs two shelters in Nassau County—Glen Cove and Long Beach—and in the wooded hills of Westchester County, a shelter at Elmsford. Here, the Society landscaped the site to match the rural setting and added a year-round aviary.

All Society shelters accept animals any time, day or night, at no charge. On request, one of the Society's 45 ambulances will make house calls to pick up unwanted animals. (Since 1954, the Society has been obliged to make a slight charge for this service except when a licensed New York City dog is involved.)

If there's any hope of finding a new home for the pet, the Society keeps the animal available as long as possible. Knowing the ways of humans as well as the ways of animals, the Society doesn't offer a pet for adoption as soon as the owner brings it in. The ASPCA holds the animal 24 hours, just in case the owner changes his mind. One man adopted a dog from a shelter, brought it back the following day, reclaimed it the next, returned it once again, then finally took it home for keeps.

The Society gives the VIP (Very Important Pet) treatment to animals going out on adoption. Nobody can guarantee an animal's health any more than tomorrow's weather; but the Society takes every precaution. It offers a free examination for each adopted pet, plus any necessary shot against communicable disease. Adopted animals altered or spayed in the Society's hospital have their own medicare plan: the owner pays only the surgical charge; the Society assumes all hospitalization, examination, entrance, drug, inoculation and other fees.

Along with the free shots and examination, the Society veterinarians give the new owner some pointers on basic animal care. For most owners, the pet they're adopting is the first they've ever had and the veterinarians stress the importance of details such as regular ear-cleaning, especially with floppy-eared dogs; dental examination; diet; exercise. This short indoctrination course isn't meant to turn the owner into a do-it-yourself veterinarian, but it does make him aware that animals, like humans, need continuing attention. In addition, the owner gets a free pamphlet on the care of his new pet.

Every adoption is a Cinderella story. A homeless animal's needs are simpler than glass slippers and pumpkin coaches, but some owners encounter more difficulties than the Prince, whose problem involved only a shoe size. Like the D'Ambrosio family, humans often have complicated requirements. In Illinois, a bedridden invalid was grief-stricken over the loss of his close companion, a black-and-white cat named Rocky. The invalid, a man named Alfred Towner, desperately wanted another cat but would only accept one that looked exactly like Rocky.

Mrs. Towner advertised for a cat of Rocky's description. Readers responded with offers of Persians, Siamese, ginger-colored cats and just about everything except what Mr. Towner insisted on: a black cat with a white belly, white feet and whiskers, a white spot under the chin, and a completely black face.

Mrs. Towner then sent a letter to the president of a cat food company in California. The executive could locate no cats like Rocky on the West Coast. Reluctantly admitting that New York might have a more varied cat population than California, he passed Mrs. Towner's letter on to a Manhattan lady, Dorothy Smith, in charge of the company's Bronze Award to outstanding cats.

Mrs. Smith did the logical thing. She called the Society. Within less than a day, Rocky's duplicate arrived at the shelter. A few hours later, a plane from La Guardia Field sped the black-and-white to her new home in Illinois. The plane undoubtedly went faster than Cinderella's coach. And it did not turn into a pumpkin.

One man who has probably seen as many Cinderella stories as anyone is Manhattan Chief Shelter Clerk Louis C. Baer. Gray-haired, wearing a pair of antique steel-rimmed spectacles, Baer looks as if he'd adopt all the animals in the shelter if he could only figure out where to keep them. When he does, the Society's adoption rate will show a marked in-

crease. Meantime, Baer helps people find the pets they want
—and sometimes the people the pets want.

Baer recalls a middle-aged woman visiting the Manhattan
Shelter not long ago. Her dog had disappeared the year before. She had grieved for him and only now felt ready to
bring a new pet into her home.

She had no particular breed in mind, no unusual requirements. Except the special sense of mutual recognition that
tells dog and human they have both come to the right place.

Baer led her through the long corridor of kennels. About
halfway, she stopped.

"Oh, I like this one," she said.

Baer could tell, from the look in the woman's eye, and the
wag in the dog's tail, that he was about to mark up another
adoption.

Suddenly a frenzied barking rose from the last kennel in
the row. Baer hurried down to investigate the uproar. In the
kennel, the dog leaped against the bars and whined so plead-
ingly that Baer asked the woman to come down.

"He acts like he wants to meet you," Baer said.

The woman stopped at the cage. "My God," she said, "he
has met me! That's my dog!"

Baer is sure the woman spoke no more than half a dozen
words and that the dog didn't even catch a glimpse of her.

The dog never revealed where he had been for the past
year, but his delighted owner forgave the prodigal and re-
adopted him immediately. She adopted the other dog, too.

A Siamese cat also regained his old home through the Society. A woman had found the animal padding along the
street one morning and brought it to the Manhattan Shelter.
With the big demand for Siamese, the Society people knew
the blue-eyed wanderer would be adopted almost immediately. But Siamese don't often figure among the strays; this
one was sleek, well cared for. The shelter workers guessed
the owner was looking for it right now.

Within an hour the telephone rang. A woman whose Siamese had just disappeared was on her way to the shelter to have a look at the new arrival.

The distraught cat-owner was platinum-haired Kim Novak, and the Siamese did indeed belong to her. He was a fellow movie star, the famous Pyewacket. Miss Novak had acquired him while making *Bell, Book and Candle.*

Pyewacket, Miss Novak explained, looking as lithe and gorgeous as her pet, must have sneaked out of the garden behind her Manhattan duplex. She was overjoyed to find him again and the Society was delighted to be of help. The only disappointment came from some of the male visitors. Seeing Miss Novak in the shelter, they had fleetingly hoped the Society was putting her up for adoption.

Mathematicians have calculated that if you give a thousand typewriters to a thousand monkeys, in the course of time one monkey will write a best-selling novel.

The same mathematical principle could apply to the Society's adoption service. Considering the constant influx, every variety of animal in the world would be bound to turn up eventually—and do so in less time than it would take the monkey to finish his novel.

Awareness of this law of probability might have been one of the ideas prompting the Society to establish its newest service: Special Adoptions.

Through Special Adoptions, applicants ask the Society to stay on the lookout for specific animals. Whether you want a Siamese or St. Bernard, the Special Adoption clerk will notify you as soon as it arrives. The waiting period depends on the animal. Salukis, Afghan hounds and Burmese cats don't appear as often as pets of less exalted ancestry. If and when they do, the Society makes sure the interested parties, pet and person, will get together.

Most recently, the Society had a horse available for adoption, the first one in about 20 years. The horse didn't have long to wait. That same day a man had stopped in at the shelter to find out about ponies. His children had been pleading for one and he wondered whether the Society ever came across any. He hadn't been thinking in terms of horses—but a horse would be twice as good.

The Society's horse had belonged to a deceased sportsman. Executors of the estate had already turned down a good many cash offers. The animal was to be a free gift to someone who knew and loved horses. The executors and the Society agreed that this applicant would be exactly right: he was a New York mounted patrolman.

The Society itself made one of the best-known adoptions: the cartoon dog Rivets, creation of artist George Sixta. The effervescent Rivets stars in a nationally syndicated newspaper strip. For some ten years now, he has also been the Society's loyal mascot, appearing on posters, booklets and in ASPCA campaigns.

Out of 23,000 adoptions, only about 500 involve larger animals such as the policeman's new horse, or tropical birds and so on. Dogs and cats, puppies and kittens, make up the majority. While most of these go to homes distinguished only by a love of animals, some adopted pets look forward to more glamorous destinies.

A prominent senator found just the pet he wanted from the Society's adoption ward. So did one of the richest businessmen in the country. Play producers don't often send out casting notices for animals, but not long ago actor Cyril Ritchard and leading lady Eileen Heckart arrived to do some special auditioning at the Manhattan Shelter.

The famous comedian and the attractive actress needed a cat to appear with them in a new play. Like all actors, Ritchard was a bit leery of having a cat on the stage. The problem was not only to find an animal that would fit the part but one that seemed, at least, a good steady sort who wouldn't upstage the humans or go pouncing on dangling backstage ropes.

A thorough professional, Ritchard is meticulous about details and wanted precisely the right kind of cat. He and Miss Heckart spent considerable time interviewing the animals and at last found one. Ritchard then began the sorting process again and picked out another.

The Society people had thought Ritchard needed only one cat for the play. The actor shook his head. "No," he said, "if this cat's going to be a star, he's entitled to an understudy!"

A future pet-owner's profession, money or social status doesn't concern the Society. Other qualities are more important and the adoption clerks have a gift for sizing up a person and tactfully discovering certain items of information:

First, whether the family is unanimous about adopting a pet. A cat-loving wife with a cat-hating husband may spark some nasty domestic quarrels, and the couple may be too occupied pitching crockery at each other to look after the cat. Experience has taught the Society that the happiest homes for animals are those in which both parents and children agree on the type of pet and sincerely want it.

Next, whether house or apartment is big enough to accommodate the pet. A Great Dane in overcrowded quarters would be miserable. So, eventually, would the humans. In the flush of enthusiasm over acquiring an animal, some people overestimate the capacity of their home and underestimate the size of the pet. In the long run, everyone will be much happier if living area and animal are in the proper proportion.

A vigorous dog needs a reasonably vigorous owner to meet the animal's high-spirited demands for exercise and amusement. The Society likes to feel sure that the prospective owner is healthy enough to cope with his new pet.

Howling, yowling and meowing are not popular sounds in crowded New York, or anywhere else. If the owner hasn't the means or inclination to give his pet attention and companionship, there isn't much point in adopting the animal at all. The Society is eager to have its animals adopted, but more eager to have them find affectionate homes.

Successful adoption means the right pet for the right person. After all, the Society's animals are among the most valuable in the world—they are, literally, priceless.

"A million dollars couldn't buy an animal from the Society," says William Mapel. "But you can get one absolutely free."

The Society doesn't charge a penny for any adopted animal. For dogs, it's necessary to pay the fee for a license, a legal requirement in New York. If the new owner wants to make a contribution, small or large, it's entirely up to him. His gift is used to help run the adoption wards.

Vice-President Mapel was standing in front of the Manhattan Shelter one spring day, enjoying an afternoon break, when a woman and a big, frisky dog emerged from the adoption center.

"He's a nice fellow," said Mapel. "Where did you get him?"

"Inside," she answered. "He's a very valuable dog. Cost me a lot of money."

"He did?" Mapel asked, raising an eyebrow. "How much?"

"They charged me fifty dollars for him," the woman said proudly.

"Listen," Mapel said confidentially, "I work for the Society and I know something about dogs. If you paid fifty dollars, you paid too much. We'd better go back and straighten this out."

"Well . . . actually it wasn't quite that much," the woman began.

Mapel is a fisherman and he approaches it with the delight that only fishermen comprehend. But unless someone needs a meal he loves to release his fish with a friendly pat and an admonition to know better next time. That day, on the pavement in front of ASPCA headquarters, Mapel was doing a little of his own brand of fishing.

"How much did it really cost?" he asked.

The woman hesitated. "Oh . . . I guess it was a lot less, maybe half of that . . ."

"Still too much," said Mapel. "Let's go inside and see those folks who sold you the dog."

The protesting woman finally admitted she had acquired the dog for no more than the price of the license. "Outside of that," she said, "I didn't have to pay anything. But if you want to know the truth, I wouldn't sell him for all the money in the world. So," she added triumphantly, "that means he's worth a whole lot more than fifty dollars!"

Mapel bowed to feminine logic. He had caught his fish and given it a friendly pat. He gallantly hailed a cab for the woman and smiled as she and her dog drove away. The Society's pets are free, but we all put our own value on animals. Some people do the same thing with diamonds.

16
The Wild Ones

Naked ladies are not a usual sight in New York—not, at least, on the street. In fact, by the time Ryan answered a call one night, the lady in question was already draped in a blue jacket which a policeman had gallantly offered. But her state of undress concerned her less than a recent episode in her shower.

"It's there!" she wailed. "I saw it! Watching me with its little beady eyes!"

One of the neighbors, her hair in curlers, tried vainly to soothe the young woman. "Now, now, Alice, don't carry on like that. You're tired, you've been working hard. Come into the house before you catch your death of cold."

The officer took Ryan aside. "She was in the shower," he said. "Claims she was scrubbing her back when some kind of snake came down off the shower curtain and climbed onto her shoulder."

"Is she sober?" Ryan asked.

"Like a judge," said the officer. "If you don't count having conniptions and five kinds of hysterics."

"What about the apartment? Did you find anything there?"

"Who, me?" said the policeman. "I don't know whether that snake's real or whether she's just seeing things, but I'm in no hurry to find out."

"You didn't go up and look?" Ryan asked.

179

"Hell no!" said the policeman. "Why do you think I called the ASPCA?"

Ryan nodded understandingly. After fifty years of rescuing animals in Manhattan, he has learned that New Yorkers occasionally see things that aren't always there. On the other hand, he has also learned that New Yorkers see things that *are* there—but have absolutely no reason to be. So, playing it safe, he took a gunny sack and a pole lasso from his car and went upstairs to investigate.

The apartment door stood open. He could hear water running. The bathroom door hung from one hinge. The young lady had evidently not worried about opening the door; her main object was to get out and Ryan was surprised she had not taken the door along with her.

He peered cautiously inside. In the bottom of the tub, under the spray of warm water, coiled a handsome 14-foot king snake, eyes closed dreamily, enjoying the bath. Although king snakes are not poisonous, this one made up for it in size. Ryan could understand why the girl got upset when it tapped her on the shoulder. A friendly gesture from a reptile that large would somehow be unconvincing.

Ryan picked up the snake, who seemed an agreeable, easygoing sort, and stowed it into the gunny sack. He went downstairs again. The girl, her neighbor and the policeman were still there, along with a large crowd.

"I won't go back," the girl was yelling. "It's waiting!"

"Everything's OK," Ryan called. "Nothing to worry about. I got him right in here." He held up the bag.

As the crowd turned its attention to Ryan, one of the passers-by asked what he had in the sack. Ryan told him. The crowd dispersed without encouragement from the policeman.

Finally persuaded there were no more reptiles on the premises, the girl allowed her neighbor to escort her upstairs. On the pavement, the policeman waited to get his coat back.

"It wouldn't have been gentlemanly," he said, "to ask for it until she got dressed. You know," he went on, "I don't figure it. How can a snake get into anybody's apartment? It can't climb through the drainpipe; it can't go up the walls and through a window. Is she maybe dating a snake charmer and he left it there by mistake?"

Ryan shrugged. "I used to wonder about those things myself. But sometimes I think it's better not to know."

Ryan has a point. There is undoubtedly an explanation for each of the unusual animals that show up in New York; but the explanation is often less plausible than the animal's being there in the first place.

At half past two one morning, Society agents went out to investigate a report that a lion was driving through Brooklyn in an automobile. They found it to be only partially accurate. The lion was riding around in a car—but he did have a human driver with him.

"I paid a lot of money for Leo," the man said, proudly patting the head of the 150-pound cub. "He likes a little ride now and then. The rest of the time, he stays in the back yard."

Since it is illegal for a private citizen to harbor a wild animal in New York, a magistrate ordered Leo turned over to the zoo. Later, when one of the Society's agents asked why he felt the necessity for keeping a lion, the man looked puzzled. "Gee, I don't know," he said. "I always wanted a lion. And it sort of dresses the place up."

Another time, the Department of Health asked the Society to keep Little Sheba, a three-month-old lioness, under observation to make sure she had a clean bill of health. In cooperation with the Department of Health, the Society does this for more than 5,000 animals a year, and it presented no problem. The Society has also sheltered many lions. Lions have been known to bite people. None of this added up to anything really out of the ordinary—except that Little Sheba belonged to the operator of a beauty salon. And the beauty salon catered exclusively to poodles. Why a lion cub should be associated with poodles is something the Society made no attempt to figure out.

Still, it is practically impossible to surprise the ASPCA. Each year, in addition to its other, more ordinary charges, the Society cares for about 4,000 offbeat animals, including alligators, skunks, bats, porcupines, raccoons, swans, ospreys, ocelots, hawks, Java temple birds, herons, mynahs, chinchillas.

Some of these arrive at one of the Society's shelters individually, some in groups. After the death of one West Side apartment dweller, the management called the Society to check on a few remaining pets.

In the apartment, ASPCA agents discovered four species of snapping turtles, tropical fish, two boa constrictors, a python, a ten-foot alligator and a man-eating piranha.

"Mr. Green," sighed the manager, advised of this small-scale zoo, "was always a great nature-lover."

Pythons, boas and alligators have not been native to New York for several million years. When they appear in the city, it's a reasonable guess that someone has deliberately brought them there, that they have escaped from zoos or pet shops, or arrived as unintentional stowaways on boats. Nevertheless, a number of wild animals do infiltrate New York under their own steam. Woods and marshes fringe some of the outlying regions of Queens, Staten Island and the Bronx. The ASPCA shelters serving these areas regularly host creatures who should feel more at home in a Disney movie.

Not long ago, a 100-pound female harbor seal showed up on Staten Island. For a temporary lodging, the Society found the most congenial place to be a bathtub. Although the seal enjoyed the tub thoroughly, the Society located more spacious quarters for her at the New York Aquarium.

Also in the Staten Island neighborhood, an owl made its way out of the woods one night and flew into an upper-floor office. Either it didn't want to or didn't know how to get out again, but in any case the office manager, next morning, discovered the bird solemnly perched on a hat rack. The Society took the owl back to the woods, hoping it would be wiser than it had been before.

"I'm up near Hastings," said one man, telephoning the Westchester shelter, "on a fishing trip. Haven't caught any fish, but I got a deer."

The ASPCA men hurried to the spot. The fisherman had been using a large net; snared in it was a 700-pound buck.

"I'd throw him back," the fisherman said desperately, "but I can't get him out of the net!"

The Society's agents disentangled the animal and the deer ran back to the woods.

"Boy," the fisherman said, "I'm sure obliged to you. I got a fishing license all right, but I'd have one hell of a time explaining that deer to the game warden!"

The Brooklyn shelter, with the responsibility of looking after animal welfare throughout an 80-square-mile area, comes in for its own share of wildlife in the form of foxes, pheasants, wild turkeys. But one recent visitor was less wild than unexpected: a brown-and-white goat.

Brooklynites noticed the goat during the height of the Christmas shopping season. Minding its own business, the goat strolled along the avenues, stopping every so often to look at the window displays. Most of the passers-by assumed that 1) the goat was part of some advertising campaign whose point, obscure at the moment, would eventually be revealed or 2) the goat had its own sound reasons for being there. Finally, one Brooklyn citizen could no longer stand the suspense and telephoned the ASPCA.

"Listen," he said, "I don't want to butt into anybody

else's business, but this goat that's walking up and down Eighth Avenue . . . I mean, is it *supposed* to be doing that?"

Santa Claus, as far as the Society knew, did not employ goats to pull his sled. Agents collected the animal and brought it back to the shelter, where the goat spent the holidays calmly.

As a matter of policy, the Society tries to return wild animals to their normal habitat. If the animal is too wild—a lion, alligator and so on—the Society finds a home for it in one of New York's several zoos. But a goat doesn't really count as a wild beast; at the same time, it's hardly the type of creature the Society normally has available for adoption by a friendly home. Not that somebody in New York wouldn't enjoy having a goat in his apartment, but the Society doubted that city life would be healthy for the goat.

At some point in its career, the goat must have had an owner. But no one arrived to claim the animal. The goat took up residence at the shelter and stayed on through New Year's. At that time, the Society had a call from a wealthy and well-known New Yorker with an estate on Long Island.

"My wife and I were talking the other day," he said, "about getting a few animals for the place. A couple of sheep, maybe. Or even a goat. I don't suppose . . . I mean, this sounds pretty silly, but you wouldn't by any chance . . ."

"Say no more," answered the shelter manager. "We do."

The goat moved to Long Island the next day and began a new life of luxury. No one ever did find out where the animal had come from. Perhaps Santa Claus had indeed been using goats that Christmas.

In Manhattan, wild animals are as routine as in the outlying shelters. Sometimes their dispositions leave much to be desired. Agent Tom Barnshaw, now retired from the Society, remembers a 150-pound chimpanzee scrambling over the ventilators in the basement of the old New York Hippo-

drome. The show was *Jumbo*, starring Jimmy Durante, and
the chimp had been hired as an extra in the animal scenes.
The theatrical life must have gone to the chimp's head. He
refused to come down from the ventilators even to sign auto-
graphs.

The chimp already held a squad of police at bay when
Barnshaw and Mark Carrigan, the Society's emergency
driver, reached the theater. Barnshaw connected a fire hose
and sprayed water in the direction of the chimp, hoping to
dampen the animal's spirits a bit and persuade it to come
down within reach.

Barnshaw gave up the water treatment when he noticed a
broken chain hanging from the simian's neck. "I'll get hold
of it and lead him down," he told Carrigan. He made a jump
for the chain.

"Do you have him?" Carrigan called.

"Hell no," Barnshaw shouted back. "He has me!" The
chimp hauled Barnshaw four feet into the air and swung him
back and forth until the ASPCA agent dropped back to
earth, pondering a new approach.

After two hours of maneuvering, the agents succeeded in
dropping a pair of lariats on the chimp, who then descended
fairly easily. But the chimp was still annoyed at Barnshaw
for spoiling his act. Before Barnshaw and Carrigan could
get the indignant actor back to his quarters, the chimp
straightened up and landed a haymaker to Barnshaw's jaw.
It was as clean a knockout as any seen in Madison Square
Garden.

When Barnshaw woke up, he thought it wiser not to come
out for the second round. He borrowed a pair of handcuffs
from one of the policemen and slipped them over the chimp's
wrists. Tied and manacled, the chimp was hustled off to his
cage. The animal's one consolation was that many human
actors had also found themselves in a similar situation.

The term "wild animal" doesn't exclude birds. One spring afternoon, Manhattan agent Joe Schlesinger was cruising through the center of town when a call came over his two-way radio to pick up a strange bird on a window ledge in the heart of the financial district.

Crowds had begun to jam the pavement by the time Schlesinger reached Wall Street. High above, at a 15th-floor window, the agent could make out a dark shape.

"It's an eagle," one of the bystanders told Schlesinger.

"Eagle, hell!" another bystander put in. "It's one of them big buzzards."

Other opinions included turkeys, South American condors and hawks. Schlesinger picked up his net and took an elevator to the building's 15th floor—a suite of law offices.

"I think it's a vulture," muttered one of the lawyers apprehensively. "They say the market's dead, but this is really going too far!"

At the lawyer's office, Schlesinger had his first close-range view of the bird: not a vulture or condor, but a rufous-necked hornbill, an Oriental bird who looks as if he tried to swallow a banana and couldn't. Rufus, as he came to be known during the two-day safari that was to follow, had a three-foot wingspread. His back and wings were a conservative gray, his tail white. His neck had a rusty-red tinge and his eyes had the shrewd, alert glance of a natural-born humorist.

Taking advantage of the cover provided by desks and swivel chairs, Schlesinger stalked closer to the window. Rufus waited until the agent poised the net, then flapped away to a neighboring building. This time, he landed on a narrow ledge 29 stories above the street.

Rufus perched there, watching with interest while Schlesinger crawled out on the ledge. Risking a glimpse downward, the ASPCA agent saw Wall Street packed solid with onlookers. It was a consoling prospect. "If I fall," Schlesinger told himself, "I can't hit the ground."

With this encouraging thought, Schlesinger took a deep breath and inched toward Rufus. The agent almost reached him, the net brushed the hornbill's tail—then Rufus took to the air.

By now, the newspapers had got wind that a man was climbing skyscrapers after a big-beaked bird. Adding to the crowd and the traffic jam stretching for blocks, came a couple of dozen photographers and reporters.

"Hey, this is great," one of the reporters cried. "Nobody's working on Wall Street. Oh, brother, wait till you see those closing prices!"

Oblivious of whatever financial havoc he might be wreaking, Rufus spread his wings and sailed from one building to the other. The hornbill had the advantage over the human from the start. Rufus didn't need to wait for elevators.

Schlesinger did. "Hey, fellows," he called as the reporters crammed into an elevator. "Hey, fellows . . ." The newsmen paid no attention. The doors of the loaded elevator closed and it departed, leaving Schlesinger on the ground floor. The ASPCA agent sighed and waited for the next one.

Toward the end of the day, Rufus lit on another window ledge just outside one big company's conference room. Schlesinger picked his way past the frantic executives.

"That bird," said the chairman ruefully, "has just broken up a million-dollar deal."

True to form, Rufus flew off just as Schlesinger was about to net him.

"I wish," added the chairman, "our board of directors could move that fast."

Dusk began falling over Wall Street. At the agent's last glimpse of Rufus, the hornbill was winging silently toward the Hudson River. Rufus was looking for a place to roost. Schlesinger packed up his net and decided to do the same.

Next morning, the Weather Bureau wondered why its

equipment had gone insane. The prediction for Manhattan and vicinity was hurricanes, followed by blizzards changing to monsoons later in the day.

"That's Rufus," said Schlesinger.

He hurried to the Weather Bureau. Thirty stories up, Rufus perched on the delicate meteorological equipment. Schlesinger borrowed a ladder, made his way to the roof and began climbing after Rufus. This time, the agent carried breakfast for the hornbill: chopped meat and cantaloupe, which is just what hornbills like.

Rufus wasn't hungry. He gave up his position at the Weather Bureau and flew to Broadway, where he and Schlesinger spent the rest of the morning.

Late in the afternoon, Rufus seemed to grow bored with the game. It was really no contest. He floated down to the top of a building and, of his own accord, walked through the open door of a pigeon coop. There Schlesinger found him waiting. Rufus made no protest when the agent picked him up and carried him to the shelter.

Rufus, in transit to a zoo, had escaped from his chaperone. The hornbill was returned safely, the stock market went back to normal, the board meetings resumed and the Weather Bureau began forecasting again. What would have happened if the door of the pigeon coop hadn't been ajar remains open to speculation.

For Ryan himself, handling wild animals is a fifty-year-old story. Usually, before he goes out on a case, he has some idea of what kind of animal he can expect to meet. But one night, when the police emergency squad called him to a well-known midtown hotel, nobody was quite sure what he would have to deal with.

"I don't know," the police inspector told him, "whether they're very big police dogs or very small wolves."

The police had already put a cordon around the front of

the hotel. Ryan stepped inside and looked around. The desk clerks had disappeared. So had the bellboys. The lobby of the hotel, one of the busiest in New York, stood deserted. Comfortably stretched out on top of the registry desk, a lean, gray shape looked back at Ryan through eyes with an oriental slant to them. On top of a filing cabinet, another animal gave Ryan a toothy grin.

The ASPCA agent ducked back into the street. "I have news for you," he said. "They're wolves."

"Yeah." The inspector nodded sadly. "I was afraid they would be."

"Where'd they come from?" Ryan asked.

"Nobody stayed around long enough to tell me very much," said the inspector. "But I think they're living here."

The wolves, as Ryan later found out, did in fact live at the hotel. A Russian trade delegation had made its headquarters there and one of the members had brought the wolves along with him. Usually, the Russian kept his pets locked up and the hotel management, not wanting to set off an international crisis, obligingly ignored the animals. That night, however, the Russians had been celebrating and, after a number of toasts in vodka, the delegate had gone off to bed. One of the room-service staff, coming to clear up the debris, took one look at the wolves and departed immediately, leaving the door wide open.

Delighted at this unexpected freedom, the wolves joyfully loped down the stairs and into the lobby. Two minutes later, they had the place to themselves.

"I've never seen so many people clear out of a building so fast," the inspector said.

Ryan estimated he could handle one wolf himself. He asked for a volunteer to help with the other one. For some years Ryan had lectured to the emergency squad on how to cope with animals, and one of his former students was in the cordon. "I'll go in with you, Ryan," he said. "You've been telling me about all this stuff. I just want to see if it works."

Ryan picked up a couple of pole lassos and the two men entered the lobby. "Don't shoot unless you have to," Ryan warned as he approached the desk. "And if you have to, try not to shoot *me*."

A moment later, Ryan dropped his lasso around one wolf's neck. Vince, the police officer, followed Ryan's example. "We got 'em," he called. "Now what do we do with 'em?"

"That's an intelligent question," Ryan said. "The first thing you do is keep a good grip on that pole."

"You don't need to tell me," Vince said.

"Then," Ryan went on, "we take them back to the guy who owns them."

"Take them back!" Vince cried. "Are you nuts?"

"Well," said Ryan, "they're his wolves, aren't they?"

With Vince following, Ryan headed for the elevator. The Russian, he had learned, lived on the sixth floor. "We better not take them both up together," he advised.

"You go in the elevator," Vince said. "I'd rather walk."

Since the elevator attendant had vacated the hotel along with everybody else, Ryan worked the controls with one hand and kept the wolf at a safe distance with the other. The animal was surprisingly obedient, but it was the longest elevator ride the ASPCA agent had ever taken.

On the sixth floor, he met Vince. One stouthearted bellboy appeared, pointed out the room and vanished again. The Russian was just waking up when Ryan and Vince stepped in.

"Dushka!" he cried. "Sachka! My little cucumbers!" The wolves frolicked around him, whining happily. Ryan still held the pole.

"Take my advice," the agent said, "get those cucumbers out of here."

The Russian looked at him in amazement. "But they hurt nobody," he protested. "They are so lovable—"

"Yeah, I can see that," Ryan said. "But suppose they change their minds?"

"No, no," the Russian insisted. "Never change minds. . . ."

"If they get out again," Ryan said, "and bite somebody, the New York police aren't going to like it. The Health Department isn't going to like it. The whole sovereign state of New York is going to be pretty upset. The Governor's going to be mad—and the Governor carries a lot of weight with the President. From there it might get into Congress and once you stir *them* up . . ."

The Russian thought for a moment. "Bad for foreign policy," he said.

"The worst," Ryan said.

The Russian nodded. "All right. You take care of them."

After a few phone calls, Ryan arranged to have the wolves boarded at the Central Park Zoo. The Russian was pleased. He could, Ryan assured him, go and visit them every day.

"Those wolves," Vince said later, "I thought they were going to give us a lot of trouble. It was a cinch."

Wolves, Ryan explained, are pack animals by nature and recognize the authority of a pack leader. Usually the leader is an older, experienced wolf, but sometimes, with wolves that are used to humans, a man can take over that position.

"Gee," said Vince, "can you imagine that! Me, the Chief Wolf!"

"Maybe this time," Ryan said. "But don't count on it. Next time, you might run into the boss himself!"

17

The Doctor in Spite of Himself

Ryan handled the Russian wolves with only a pole lasso and a pair of gloves. Nevertheless, special devices can sometimes help in rescue work. Ryan has invented much of this equipment himself.

Early in his career, Ryan figured out a way to improve the horse-slings then in use. With his design, one man can now put a sling on a horse in the space of one minute and the horse stays comfortable and secure. Ryan has used this one-minute sling to fish horses out of cellars, rivers, building excavations and a dozen other places where you would least expect to find a horse. Many of the humane societies throughout the world have standardized on Ryan's design.

Horses are not the only ones who get in tight spots. During World War II, Civil Defense people realized that on top of the possibility of having to cope with millions of frantic humans during an air raid, they would very likely have to cope with millions of animals—of all sizes, shapes and species.

At that time, in the Society's special Animal Aid classes, Ryan added lecturing and demonstrating to his duties. He taught volunteers how to muzzle an injured dog, how to apply emergency splints and, in general, how to handle panicky animals during an air attack. Ryan showed his students how to tether horses caught on the street during an alert and, in case of air attack, suggested giving horses their feed bags whether it was mealtime or not. First, it would make sure that the animals had enough to eat in case they stayed unattended for any long period.

"And," Ryan added, "eating helps take their mind off their troubles."

If the noise from exploding bombs should get too loud, Ryan also suggested a simple, homely remedy: putting cotton in a pet's ears.

"There's not much else you can do," Ryan said. Animals' ears are much more sensitive than people's and the cotton would, at least, damp out some of the sound and shock. "It should work pretty good with humans, too," Ryan advised.

As for animals marooned on rooftops or upper stories of buildings, Ryan, in cooperation with the Civil Defense people, adapted some of the principles of his horse-sling for the use of smaller creatures.

But a good many of Ryan's inventions date from long before World War II. Like the horse-sling, Ryan's version of the pole lasso for dogs has been a standard piece of humane equipment for more than a quarter of a century.

Aside from his inventions, Ryan has increased his arsenal with such humble items as onion bags, gunny sacks, balls of yarn and snakes (the flexible metallic kind that plumbers use).

Ryan finds plumbers' snakes ideal for helping cats out of drainpipes and sewer catch basins. A good many times, the cat isn't actually trapped but simply too scared to move; in which case, Ryan soaks a gunny sack with sardine oil, attaches it to the end of the snake and inserts the whole business into the pipe. Then, like any cat-owner playing with his pet, Ryan wiggles the snake back and forth to lure the cat out. The sardine oil helps. It would take a determinedly disinterested cat to ignore the temptation.

Cats often wind up in chimneys—and this is where the onion bags come in. Baited with liver or fish, the loosely woven, netlike bags entangle the cat's paws just long enough for Ryan to drop a loop of rope under the forelegs and hoist the cat up gently.

The cat-pole which Ryan uses for bringing distraught cats out of trees is based on an item of grocery store equipment not to be found in today's supermarkets. Ryan, in fact, got his inspiration for the pole from a grocery store where he and his young bride, May, had gone shopping.

Ryan had just come out of the army at the close of World War I, had returned to his work with the Society and had somehow managed to find time to get married. The newly-weds were in the midst of buying provisions when May noticed a rapt expression on her husband's face.

"Look at that," Ryan whispered as the grocery clerk, armed with a pole, reached up for a box of cereal. "Suppose that box of cornflakes was a cat."

"If that box of cornflakes was a cat," May answered, "you'd have a big surprise for your breakfast."

Women, Ryan decided, could not follow an obvious line of reasoning. He said no more about it, but for the next few evenings set about redesigning the grocery pole and trans-forming it into a fool proof cat-rescuing device. In place of the bare metal clamps, Ryan used a comfortable, padded, collarlike arrangement. He also added some new wrinkles that would make the action smoother and more effective.

Eventually, the gadget was perfected and, like others of Ryan's inventions, became standard in many different coun-tries. But he put so much time on it that May, already re-signed to being an ASPCA widow, could only be thankful they hadn't shopped for groceries during their honeymoon.

In addition to his inventions, Ryan has been known to dab-ble a bit in veterinary medicine. William Mapel, the Society's Administrative Vice-President, enjoys ribbing Ryan about practicing without a license. Ryan indignantly protests that he only administers first aid. But Ryan's first aid, especially in the days before the Society developed its current staff of veterinarians, has probably saved more animal lives than anyone could reckon.

Ryan has a healthy respect for veterinary medicine—as long as it works; and while he admires the new wonder drugs, he has never forgotten how to use remedies handed down through generations of horse handlers. His private pharmacy includes turpentine, carbolic acid, oakum, collodion, iodoform, bicarbonate of soda. Ryan also gives the impression of knowing so much about herb-lore and horse-lore that, if he had to, he could gather his own raw materials in Central Park. One of his basic ingredients is whiskey. "For horses," Ryan says. "I never touch the stuff."

With his first-aid methods, Ryan has eased horses suffering from lockjaw by rigging up complicated wick arrangements to keep their mouths and throats moist. Using a perforated pipe, Ryan has bathed animals to reduce fever. He knows how to neutralize stomach acid, empty a horse's colon —procedures which can be lifesaving if applied promptly. Ryan has worked on animals in the middle of the day or night, winter and summer, in deserted neighborhoods or in the middle of a Manhattan street. Usually, the bystanders don't have the vaguest idea what he's doing—except that he seems to be helping the animal. But he also has a stack of letters from people who have written to the Society, praising the man's amazing skill.

Once, Ryan had a call to go to Sixth Avenue, where a grocery-wagon horse had fallen in the street. As soon as he examined the animal, Ryan knew it was suffering from azoturia, a condition of too much nitrogen in the urine. One of the horse's hind legs had already started to be paralyzed. Ryan administered a shot of colic medicine, emptied the horse's bowels and wrapped the animal in blankets. Then he called for the Society's horse ambulance to deliver the patient to the grocery company's stable, where a contract veterinarian could take over.

Ryan had been pretty busy during the course of all this, but when he had finished and stopped to catch his breath, he noticed an elderly man watching him with interest. Shabbily dressed, he carried a blanket roll over his shoulder.

"You done all right there," the man called. "What's wrong with that horse, anyway?"

"You a country boy?" Ryan asked. "Ever hear of black-water?"

The man nodded. He questioned Ryan about what would eventually happen to the horse, and what kind of treatment the animal would get. Ryan, who makes a policy of giving polite answers to all queries, no matter how unlikely the source, explained it in detail. "That horse is going to come around all right," Ryan added. "I know it."

The man nodded again. "That horse belonged to a big company," he said. "What about a poor man's animal?"

Ryan assured him it would get the same treatment as a millionaire's.

"But what if that poor man can't pay?" the man asked.

"If he can't pay," Ryan said, "he doesn't have to. The Society won't charge him a nickel."

"Interesting," mused the bystander. "Very interesting."

The man disappeared into the crowd then and Ryan thought no more of him. That afternoon, Ryan was ordered to report to the Society's General Manager, William K. Horton.

When Ryan entered Horton's office, the manager asked if he had been the agent handling the grocery-wagon horse on Sixth Avenue. Ryan admitted that he was, casting back in his mind to remember what he could conceivably have done wrong.

"Don't look so nervous, Ryan," Horton told him. "Nobody's going to shoot you. A friend of yours stopped in a little while ago. He left this for you." The manager tossed over a

wad of ten-dollar bills. "There's fifty of them," Horton
added.

Ryan stared at the money. "A thin fellow, needed a shave?
Carried a blanket roll?"

"The same," Horton said.

Ryan shook his head. "I can't keep this," he said. "Poor
devil, it must have been his life savings. Put it in the ambulance fund, it'll do more good there."

"Not a chance," Horton said. "This is yours. He made that
very clear. Besides, you deserve it. You really sold him on the
Society, and any salesman's entitled to his commission."

"I still think . . ." Ryan began. "The Society . . ."

"I told you he left it for you," Horton said. "Oh, as far as
the Society's concerned"—the manager held up another
sheaf of ten-dollar bills—"there's a hundred of them here.
That's what he left for us."

"Say," Ryan cried, "who is this guy?"

Horton shrugged. "I don't know. That's one thing he
wouldn't tell us."

Ryan pieced out some more of the story later on. As one
of the other agents told him, his unknown benefactor had
stalked into the Society's headquarters demanding to see
somebody in charge. Ushered into Horton's office, the mysterious donor proceeded to haul up his shirt and pull fifteen
hundred dollars out of an old money belt. He was loaded
with money, said the agent, not only in the money belt but in
his pockets, pinned inside his clothes, in the waistband of his
trousers. When Horton presented a receipt for the donation,
the man smiled, thanked him, tore up the slip of paper,
dropped it into the wastebasket and hurried out into the
street.

Ryan often speculated as to who the fellow might have
been: a Texas oilman in disguise, the black sheep of some
prominent family, a bookie on the lam, a bank robber with

pangs of conscience, an eccentric scientist with a valuable patent? Whoever it was, he liked animals—which, in Ryan's opinion, makes up for a multitude of sins.

If Ryan is not averse to practicing a little veterinary medicine under the guise of first aid, he is just as willing to administer medical treatment to himself. Even Ryan is not 100 percent infallible in his work with animals, and in the course of fifty years has been kicked, scratched and nipped; he has been bitten perhaps twenty times, a gratifyingly low average when spread over half a century. In the bite cases, however, there was always the danger of rabies, and doctors have talked themselves hoarse imploring him to get anti-rabies shots.

Ryan, who has never had rabies in his life, has always refused. He prefers an old standby remedy he has used for years, a three-part prescription consisting of the following:

1. One drop of carbolic acid on the wound
2. Ten seconds later, one drop of sterile alcohol on top of the carbolic
3. One Irish jig, danced *ad libitum*. This last is optional, but according to Ryan it passes the time while you're waiting for the pain of Parts 1 and 2 to go away.

"Damn it all, Ryan," a doctor told him, "I don't see how you can get by with that. If it was anybody else, I'd say they were too mean to catch anything. In your case, you're either immune—or just plain lucky."

Ryan has done more than patch cuts and bruises and treat himself for rabies. Going out to investigate an unlicensed airedale one day, the Ryan persuasiveness either ran into a dry spell or the dog was too grumpy to appreciate it. The airedale ended up not only biting Ryan but breaking his little finger.

After the carbolic-acid treatment, complete with jig-dancing, Ryan set his own finger, splinted it with pieces of an old egg basket and tied it up with friction tape. But the splint soon bothered him and finally he threw it away. The finger showed no sign of damage.

Some months later, on an errand to Bellevue Hospital, one of the technicians called him into the X-ray room.

"Come on, Ryan," said the technician, "I'm practicing. Put your mitt in the fluoroscope and let's have a look at it."

As soon as the technician saw Ryan's finger through the machine, he called one of the residents to see it.

The doctor shook his head in admiration. "Boy, I've never seen a break like that knit so well. It's perfect. Who did that work?"

"I had a real good man for that one," Ryan said.

The doctor nodded. "I should think so. Which bone surgeon was it?"

"Well," Ryan said, "I don't think you could call him a bone surgeon. He was more of a horse doctor."

13

3 R's for Animals

Ryan is really too big and muscular for anyone to believe he counts the Little People among his ancestors—although that could be one explanation for his skill not only as a do-it-yourself doctor, but an animal handler. Certainly a portion of his way with animals has come down through generations. Another part stems from meeting bulls and bears (the real kind), horses, dogs and elephants practically every day of his life. But to a lot of city people, even a hamster may seem as strange and remote as a Martian; a city child's contact with animals often consists only of Disney movies, TV cartoons or a quick trip through the zoo.

Teaching children to appreciate animals not as comic characters but as living creatures is an important part of any educational system. The average teacher doesn't say, "Now, children, turn to page three in your turtle" or "Jimmy, would you mind reading the first paragraph of the chinchilla?" But this, figuratively, is what happens at one of New York's most unusual schools. Each year, in a spacious classroom at the Manhattan Shelter, more than 16,000 children (and adults) attend the Society's Humane Education lectures and demonstrations. The living textbooks include dogs, cats, mice, and almost 200 technicolor tropical birds.

In the class, a blind girl strokes the long, silky ears of a rabbit and laughs with delight at her discovery. A deaf child sees what friendship looks like from the wagging tail of a dog.

200

A boy whose only handicap is shyness about greeting the Society's tame boa constrictor finally ventures to touch the handsome reptile.

"Let the child learn," said Henry Bergh, "that there is no being so insignificant as to be unworthy of protection, be it the worm which crawls upon the ground."

Bergh saw clearly that the long-term success of the humane movement depended on education. He himself took to the lecturing platform, wrote newspaper and magazine articles. He printed and distributed literature at his own expense, one of the earliest being a small pamphlet entitled *Our Dumb Chattels.* In 1873, Bergh published a monthly magazine, *The Animal Kingdom,* a title later changed to *Our Animal Friends.* Designed for young readers, it carried material by some of the most prominent authors of the day, including Harriet Beecher Stowe and Louisa May Alcott.

Today, the Society publishes two attractive periodicals: *Animal Protection* and the *ASPCA News Bulletin.* The Humane Education Department has also prepared a series of animal-shaped bookmarks carrying information on the care of dogs, cats, turtles, hamsters, guinea pigs, horses, mice, rats, rabbits, fish and parakeets. Each year, the Society distributes about 8,000 calendars with animal pictures.

Most popular on the list of the Society's animal-care booklets are, naturally, those about dogs and cats: *That New Puppy, Your Dog and His Care,* and *Cats and Their Care.* But Manhattan pet shops report an unprecedented demand for snakes—the bigger and more exotic the better. The Society doesn't offer a pamphlet on Training Your New Python, and the reptile boom may be a passing phenomenon, but if it grows, and enough people show interest in such a booklet, the Humane Education Department will gladly oblige.

The Society distributes about 59,000 pieces of educational literature every year. Public schools receive it free; the public can buy it at cost; prices for booklets range from a nickel to 35 cents.

And, of course, anyone who adopts a pet from the Society gets a free copy of the booklet dealing with that particular animal. In addition, the Society offers a selection of film strips and other visual aids; every year, more than 500 schools, pet clubs, civic groups and humane societies use this ASPCA material to reach an audience of almost 18,000.

The Humane Education Department's library holds hundreds of volumes of animal reference books, as well as the better fiction featuring animals as central characters. Staff members, however, don't confine educational activities to the printed page. Within any given year, they make an average of 39 public appearances, lecturing and demonstrating animal care on radio and TV, in schools and to teen-age organizations. The Humane Education Department also gives lecture-demonstrations at the New York Public Library.

But if one picture is worth a thousand words, one live animal must be worth a thousand pictures. One of the most exciting attractions is the classroom on the third floor of the Manhattan Shelter. Some years ago, Society demonstrators had to make do mainly with stuffed animals. Now, immaculate cages with live tenants line the walls, giving the impression of a miniature zoo. The Society's big, flamboyant macaw acts as official greeter.

Much of the credit for the switch from stuffed specimens to the present contingent of live models goes to the Society's former President, Hugh Paine, and ASPCA General Manager, the late Warren McSpadden, the two men who sparked the idea of the Animalport for animal air travelers at Idlewild. McSpadden's background as a science teacher and school supervisor gave him unusual insights into the art of capturing a child's imagination. He produced movies and developed instruction courses. A first-rate photographer, he also provided the Society's publications with spectacular shots of animal life.

The Department's present supervisor is a vivacious young lady named Diana Henley. She has such a widely diversified assortment of talents that the amazing thing ceases to be their number and variety—but that she has been able to find a focus for all of them in the Society.

Miss Henley, with a Bachelor of Arts degree from UCLA, has studied acting, teaching, worked in little theater, written several books—and has loved animals since childhood. Every other week, she packs up a monkey, mynah or one of the department's other animals and does a guest shot on one of the children's TV programs. She lectures, writes some of the Society's animal-care literature, and serves as consultant on animal problems to a number of organizations, including one of the big insurance companies. Since life insurance companies are more concerned with the health and longevity of their human clients, no one would expect them to be much involved with animal care. Nevertheless, the company felt information of this type to be a public service and turned to the ASPCA for advice and guidance. The result, gained through the Society's cooperation plus some hard work by Miss Henley and the Humane Education Department, was a bright and knowledgeable series of booklets on pets.

Organizing and conducting programs for children account for a large part of the Humane Education Department's effort. The resident animal faculty helps out, too.

Most educational institutions recruit their professors through the usual academic channels. At the Society, furred or feathered members of the teaching staff arrive with a background far removed from hallowed halls of ivy. Some are unclaimed strays whose origins will remain forever a mystery. Others are gifts to the Society—gifts which the giver is usually delighted and relieved to unload.

"A lot of people like the idea of keeping exotic pets," Miss Henley says. "After a while, they realize these animals are terrifically hard to care for properly."

The kinkajou or Cebus monkey that looked like such fun in the pet shop just doesn't seem to work out right in a Manhattan apartment. Often the disillusioned owner donates his exotic friend to the Society.

The Humane Education Department's most startling faculty member, the big boa constrictor, has the strangest background of all. After matriculating in the jungle, taking advanced courses in camouflage and tree-draping, he suddenly appeared in a New York Post Office during the height of the Christmas rush.

The boa had no passport, no package or shipping instructions. He didn't have a stamp to qualify for first-class mail or even parcel post. Desperate clerks called the Society to take charge. Miss Henley guesses that the boa was originally destined for a zoo. On the other hand, he might have been on some obscure business of his own, perhaps even an exchange fellowship. Whatever his history, he has been teaching at the Society for the past five years.

The word "teaching" is not used here facetiously. Interpreted through their human supervisor, the lessons animals have to teach are meaningful to every child visiting the Society's classroom. First, youngsters learn that strange and even frightening animals turn out to be friends.

The boa is the best example. When Miss Henley first brings out the big reptile, many of her young students gasp at the sight. Some of them shriek when she drapes the boa about her shoulders or winds it around her waist as a 100 per cent authentic snakeskin belt—with the snake still enclosed.

Some anthropologists believe that humans possess a deep-rooted fear of snakes, deriving from our simian connections; others say it comes mainly as a result of social conditioning.

From what Miss Henley has observed, the biggest factor is inexperience. It's a lot easier to like the animals you see most frequently.

Eventually, most of the children get up enough nerve to stroke the boa. When they do, their doubts change to delighted amazement. Snakes, they suddenly find out, aren't damp and slimy at all. Instead, they feel slightly cool, smooth and as pleasant to the hand as a bolt of silk.

Mice make wonderful mothers, the children learned from one maternal mouse that undertook raising her deceased colleague's litter. And, although the Society hasn't a lion and lamb to lie down together, the Humane Education Department does have a guinea pig and turtle that are the closest of friends. The cat and dog enjoy each other's company—thereby demolishing at least one old-wives' tale. Harmony among animals certainly suggests that human beings can get along with each other, too.

The most important thing the children learn in the Society's classroom is love and respect for animals. A child who has had the pleasure of cuddling a milkweed-soft chinchilla or listening to the affectionate rumble of a purring cat stands a good chance of taking some of this warmth back with him into his daily life. Communication, with or without words, is the beginning of understanding. Between children and animals this happens quickly, and the good feeling may last a lifetime.

Animals also help break down other serious barriers. In recent years, the Humane Education Department has made a practice of inviting groups of emotionally disturbed children from New York's well-known League School. Sometimes a hamster or white rabbit accomplishes what trained teachers and psychiatric workers have tried fruitlessly to achieve. An emotionally disturbed child, withdrawn into a world of silence and loneliness, too terrified to speak to adults or other children, will very often talk to an animal. A breakthrough like that may open the way to more effective therapy.

The Humane Education Department enriches the classroom sessions with a grand tour of the hospital. Favorite stopping-point for the kids is the Society's dog and cat adoption wards. No one can estimate exactly how many young visitors have gone home later, bursting with what they've seen, to apply some not-so-subtle pressure on their parents to get one of the Society's puppies or kittens. It probably happens frequently, but so far no parent has kicked. Happily, love for animals is contagious.

A trip through a candy-making plant wouldn't be complete without a free sample. The Society follows the same principle, although it doesn't hand out samples indiscriminately. Partly through choice, partly through the workings of inexorable biological laws, the Humane Education Department has taken on a sideline: breeding hamsters, parakeets and white mice. Any school group promising to care for it may adopt one of the little animals.

Schoolchildren and their teachers visit the classroom on weekdays, while Saturdays are reserved for the Society's Junior Members. Any young person under eighteen may join as an individual; and the Society welcomes Scouts, Campfire Girls, Y members and so on to join as a group.

The Juniors go about animal welfare more thoroughly than the weekday visitors, and many plan to become veterinarians. Juniors help conduct tours, feed the animals and walk the faculty dog; they also learn first aid from the Society's own veterinarians. Bandaging a dog or giving a pill to a cat can be a harrowing experience for adults, but the Juniors acquire these arts easily—and the demonstrator animals are good-natured about the whole procedure.

Juniors with 50 hours of service in a year win the Society's

Junior Achievement Award, an honor presented at the Jamboree held in Central Park each June.

Like all teachers, the Humane Education Department learns from its students. One thing the staff has discovered: the traditional picture of a boy inseparable from his dog is a little misleading.

"Girls," says Diana Henley, "are much more devoted, much more enthusiastic animal lovers, than boys."

The girls are more eager to meet new animals, are willing to work harder in caring for them—and aren't half as scared. When Diana Henley invites her young pupils to drape the boa constrictor around their necks, the first volunteer is almost invariably a girl.

Teaching humans how to get along with animals is one part of the Humane Education Department's job. The other is teaching animals how to get along with humans.

In any big city, especially New York, an untrained dog on the streets can be a bigger traffic hazard than a woman shopper. The compulsive yapper, nipper, or Great Dane that loves to jump up on people rapidly forfeits the role of man's best friend and gains a reputation as a complete lout. To help dogs and their owners avoid this situation, the Society offers obedience training courses at the Manhattan, Brooklyn and Glen Cove Shelters.

The program began in 1944; since then, 18,000 dogs and their owners have attended the Society's classes. Blanche Saunders, the famous dog trainer who brought the idea of formal training from England and who sparked much of the enthusiasm for it in this country, was the ASPCA's training instructor for 17 years. Charles Leedham is now in charge.

Obedience training involves more important matters than teaching a dog to give you his paw. Freshmen learn to heel, lie down, come when you call them and, equally important, to stay put when you tell them to. Upperclassmen go deeper into these subjects and do some advanced work in carrying and retrieving. The question comes up: Who's being trained, the owner or the dog?

"The owner," answers Diana Henley. "Mr. Leedham and his helpers train *you* to train your dog."

In the process, human and animal must first establish a mutual vocabulary. The owner must be consistent in using command words and gestures. The dog gradually learns what's expected of him—and the owner learns what he can expect from his dog.

Dogs generally do their best to please their owners. They look for leadership and direction; like children, they feel more secure in the presence of a reliable authority.

Almost everyone, the Society has found, can learn to train a dog; although it's true that some people learn a little faster than others and some have a natural flair for it.

"Theater people," says Miss Henley, "actors and dancers, make some of the best dog handlers. They're trained to use their bodies and voices, to develop stage presence and project their personalities. They have an excellent sense of timing, which is very important in obedience training."

Miss Henley has had plenty of opportunity to observe this. Many theater people bring their animals to the ASPCA courses and Miss Henley has helped train the dogs of celebrities such as actress Sylvia Sidney, the musical comedy star Gwen Verdon, and singer Leslie Uggams.

It's also true that some dogs learn faster than others. Breed doesn't seem to have much bearing on the matter—with a few possible exceptions. Hounds, in Miss Henley's experience, are a little harder to train. They're usually good-natured, easygoing characters who somehow just don't take the idea of training very seriously. Few things in life are really urgent, as far as a hound is concerned. Beagles and dachshunds share much of this attitude.

Working dogs approach their training in a competent, businesslike manner and usually make excellent students. Obedience and cooperation with humans have run in their family for centuries, and these traits show up to good advantage in the Society's courses. Among the easiest dogs to train are poodles. Most often, they're smart, quick to catch on to what the owner wants. (Some poodle fanciers feel that their dogs are on a level with telepaths and mind readers.) Like seals, poodles love an audience and respond strongly to praise.

"They're really terrible hams," says Miss Henley.

Still, there's no predicting which individual dog will do best in training. Sometimes the most unlikely candidates graduate *summa cum laude*. The Society acquired a Chihuahua, brought to the Manhattan Shelter as an abandoned animal. The little creature had obviously been mistreated, was frightened and cowering. Miss Henley adopted the dog, worked patiently to gain its friendship and confidence. The Chihuahua did so well that eventually it became a demonstration dog.

In its eight-week course, the Society covers the basic points of good canine behavior. Some applicants, fascinated by one New York department store's use of dogs as night watchmen, or perhaps carried away by the adventures of the Army's K-9 Corps, ask to have their pets taught combat techniques.

The answer is always a polite "No." The Society does not give attack training. In the Society's opinion, a dog trained for this purpose is, in the hands of an amateur, more dangerous than a loaded gun.

Instead, the obedience courses emphasize a good working —and loving—relationship between dog and owner. The training isn't harsh or overdemanding for animal or human.

"Sometimes," Miss Henley says, "obedience training can mean a real blossoming for the dog."

It can mean a blossoming for the owner, too. The Society

has never offered obedience training courses with the fringe benefit of teaching an owner how to win friends and influence people. But things often work out that way. The owners acquire a confidence in dealing with their pets that carries over into their dealings with people.

Miss Henley recalls one young woman, attractive but painfully shy, who seemed at first incapable of ordering a fly off a tablecloth. During the classes, her whole personality changed. She turned out to be a brilliant handler—and an exceptional person in her own right. Developing her pet's abilities helped the girl develop her own.

This Dale Carnegie type of success story is a bonus. Most owners are less concerned about influencing people than influencing their dogs. But, whichever way it works out, a glamorous new career or a well-mannered cocker spaniel, the Humane Education Department is pleased. So is the owner. So is the cocker spaniel.

19

The Stray and the Soprano

Despite the high enrollments in the Society's obedience classes, New York's dog population is going to the dogs. In 1954, there were almost 280,000 licensed dogs; most recently, that figure has dropped by about 25,000. A lot of New York City families have been moving to the suburbs, taking their pets with them. A number of the new housing developments won't allow dogs on the premises. These are probably the two main reasons for the decrease. But even the reduced number of dogs still gives the Society an expensive problem.

In 1894, the State Legislature empowered the ASPCA to issue dog licenses in New York City and collect the fees involved. At the time, the arrangement seemed fair enough. The Society used the money to defray the costs of supplying tags, handling all the administrative work, returning lost dogs to their owners, and maintaining shelters for lost, strayed or homeless animals. ASPCA services embrace far more than what is attendant to dog licensing. The licensing operation, however, up till 1963, had come to be a serious drain on the Society's resources. Whereas it always was contemplated that the ASPCA at least would break even on operating the dog license franchise for the City of New York, in 1962 the Society's deficit on this operation alone was $195,600; its aggregate deficit since 1956 on the dog tag business had been $953,400 the beginning of the 1963–64 fiscal year.

On top of everything else, the Society knows that the most rigid economy cannot reduce annual expenses for all operations below nearly $2,000,000. With some $70,000 worth of charity treatments, the ASPCA hospital loses substantially more than $160,000 a year, and Humane Work and Humane Education, neither of which produces income, have operational costs upwards of $150,000 a year.

Income from the Society's portfolio and from annual memberships and contributions appropriately can be applied toward financing the humane activities of the ASPCA. Over the last half dozen years, however, the drain of the dog-licensing deficit has been more than the Society could bear. That is why it became so necessary to go to the New York State Legislature in January, 1963, for relief through an increase in the dog license fee.

Aside from issuing dog tags, the concomitants of the license service alone have been more than money can buy. Within a single year the Society returned 5,788 lost dogs not only to New Yorkers but to owners in Florida, California, and all over the United States. In one case, the Society received a letter from a man in Buenos Aires, Argentina, advising that he had found a dog with an ASPCA license. Checking its cross-index, the Society learned the dog's owner still lived in New York.

The ASPCA contacted the amazed New Yorker, who explained that his dog had strayed during a trip to South America. He had given up hope of finding the animal again. The Society arranged for the 6,000-mile trip from Buenos Aires; owner and pet had a happy reunion at the boat.

Most dog-owners would agree that this can't be calculated in dollars. Yet if a dog is supposed to be a man's best friend, sometimes it doesn't always seem that way. It did not seem that way at all the night Ryan had a call from the police department about a small riot taking place in an apartment house near 137th Street.

The police reported hearing yells and calls for help, and seeing miscellaneous objects flying through a window. To Ryan, it sounded like nothing more serious than an ordinary domestic squabble. "What," he asked, "does that have to do with the Society? If a man's beating an animal, that's one thing. If he's beating his wife, that's something else."

"I don't know who's doing what to who," said the officer. "But this is Society business. There's one hell of a big dog in that apartment."

"How do you know?" Ryan asked. "Did you go in to find out?"

"Go in?" said the policeman. "That dog won't let us go in. Every time we try to turn the doorknob, he grabs it with his mouth."

"Don't put me on," Ryan said. "You're a grown man. A dog can't stop you from opening a door."

"I told you," said the officer, "this is a *big* dog. I looked at him through the keyhole. Until he started looking back at *me*."

Hurrying to 137th Street, Ryan found the squad car, two policemen and the building superintendent. None of them seemed eager to invade the apartment.

"All right," Ryan told the superintendent, "you take this flashlight. Shine it on the fire escape. I'm going to climb up." He turned to the policemen. "You boys," he said, "go to the apartment. When you hear me come in the window, you go through the door."

Ryan clambered onto the narrow iron ladder and made his way up three flights. Peering through the bedroom window, he saw nothing at first. After a moment, a white Eskimo dog came and sat on the bed and looked curiously at the ASPCA agent. The police had been right. It was a big dog. A very big dog. Ryan was only surprised that the dog hadn't opened the door and tossed the policemen down the stairs.

"Good boy," Ryan said hopefully. He slowly raised the window.

Instead of running toward him, the dog raced into the living room and dove under the sofa. At the same moment, the policemen burst into the apartment. Ryan met them in the foyer.

The rooms were empty and silent. "Hey," said one of the policemen, "you don't think the dog was throwing all that stuff out the window?"

"I don't know," Ryan said. "Some of these huskies are pretty smart."

A loud yell came from the bathroom. Both policemen drew their guns.

"Take it easy," Ryan said. "If the dog's that smart, maybe he's got a friend in there."

The police sidled up to the door, kicked it open and jumped back. Inside, Ryan saw a man and a woman standing petrified in the bathtub.

"My God," cried the man, with relief, "I thought you'd never get here!"

For the past hour, the man explained, he and his wife had been pitching medicine bottles, hairbrushes and tubes of toothpaste, trying to get attention.

"Didn't you think the phone would have worked better?" asked Ryan.

"Phone!" the man exclaimed. "We couldn't get to the phone. Mukluk wouldn't let us!'"

The man and his wife had taken Mukluk with them to visit a local bar. Back at the apartment, Mukluk had turned playful; so playful that he had begun chasing the couple all over the place.

"Every time we tried to move," the husband said, "he'd jump on us. When we tried to get into the hall, he stood in front of the door. He acted like it was a big joke. Finally, he chased us into the bathroom."

"I think he's lost his mind," the woman put in.

Ryan thought for a moment. "Listen," he said. "When you were at the bar did Mukluk have anything to drink?"

"Well . . ." The man hesitated. "He might have had a little. He acted thirsty. I bought him a couple of beers."

"That," said Ryan, "was about the stupidest thing you could have done. The dog isn't out of his mind. He's drunk!"

The effect of the beer had begun to wear off, for Mukluk now crawled from under the sofa and wagged his tail at Ryan.

"Besides the drinks," Ryan asked, "did you give him anything else?"

"No," said the man, "only a couple of sausages, a hard-boiled egg and some potato chips—just the snacks at the bar, the same as we had."

Ryan warned the owner that overloading a dog's stomach could throw the animal into running fits. He advised taking Mukluk to a veterinarian in the morning.

"Morning?" said the wife. "You think I'm going to stay in the bathroom all night? You take him. He's all yours."

The couple agreed that Mukluk, drunk or sober, was too much for them to cope with. "Suppose he thought this was fun?" the man asked. "Suppose he wants to try it again?"

Ryan took Mukluk back with him and, in the morning, entered the husky in the adoption service.

Mukluk did not have long to wait. He was a handsome dog and several requests came for him almost immediately. Ryan was convinced Mukluk had found a good home. The man who finally adopted him was a teetotaler.

Admitting dogs to be one of man's best friends, the reverse is not necessarily true. In civilian clothes, walking through the Times Square neighborhood one cold evening, Ryan noticed a man standing on a street corner. The man was wrapped in an overcoat, scarf and earmuffs. Shivering in front of him stood four of the scrawniest poodles Ryan had ever seen.

The ASPCA agent walked over to the man. "Mister," Ryan asked, "what do you think you're doing with those dogs?"

The man gave him a hard look. "What's it look like I'm doing? I'm not out here for my health. I'm selling these mutts."

Ryan put his hands on his hips. "If you want to know something," he said, "I don't give a damn about your health. If you want to freeze all night, that's your business. Don't wish it on the dogs."

From the crowd of passers-by, one well-dressed woman pulled her escort over to the curb. "Oh, Charlie, look at the poor doggies." She bent and patted one on the head.

"The outcasts from a broken home, ma'am," the poodle dealer said sorrowfully. "They got no place to go. I promised to do my best for them."

"Charlie, I want one," the woman pleaded. "They're so cold and miserable we can't leave them here . . ."

The poodle-peddler went on with his pitch. The dogs, he explained, belonged to a well-known actress in the process of breaking up with her husband. The poodles had to be disposed of somehow.

"If they belonged to *her*," said the woman, "we've *got* to buy one."

"Lady," Ryan interrupted, "if you want to give a dog a home, I'm with you. But don't fall for that line of—"

"Only twenty-five dollars," the peddler put in hastily. "You can't find another pedigreed animal in New York for that kind of money."

"That's for damned sure," Ryan said.

"Come on," the woman's escort insisted, "we're late for the show." He finally managed to detach her from the dogs and they moved away.

"Get out of here," the peddler ordered. "You busted that sale for me. Who do you think you are?"

Ryan pulled out his badge. "You can sell all the dogs you

want," he said, "if anybody's dumb enough to believe that malarkey. But you aren't going to freeze them before you sell them."

"Don't tell me my business," the peddler said. "These people don't want a happy mutt. They go for the other kind. It makes them feel like they're doing something noble. The colder the dog looks, the higher the price."

"You take those dogs back where you got them," Ryan said. "If you don't, I'll make you a promise: you'll be talking to a judge before the night's over."

"All right, already," the man protested. "Later, later."

"Take them back now," Ryan said. "I'll make you another promise. I'll check every street corner in New York if I have to—to make good and sure you do it."

The man gathered up the animals and moved away. Ryan was as good as his word. That night and for the next few evenings, he patrolled the entire area. There was no sign of the peddler. Toward the end of the week, Ryan did come across him again. He was still peddling poodles. But they were much smaller, made in Japan, with a wind-up key in the back.

"Hey, wise guy!" the peddler called. "You got anything to say about this?"

"No," Ryan answered. "That's out of my department."

The mechanical poodles whirred and trotted over the pavement. The peddler, Ryan saw, didn't seem too unhappy about the changeover. His prices for the Japanese toys were a lot lower than those he charged for the live ones, but Ryan figured the peddler made up for it on volume. You buy one, Ryan thought, and two hours later you want to buy another.

The police have their problems, too.

"Tonight," said one of Ryan's patrolmen friends, "we're going to pick up the Bomber."

"Which one?" Ryan asked.

"How do I know?" said the policeman. "All they tell me is a lot of complaints have been coming in. There's this woman," he went on, "been showing up in Central Park every night. Man on Fifth Avenue saw her twice. Couple of the cabbies flagged her, too. They say she's got a package with her. Takes it into the bushes and that's it. She leaves it there and disappears."

"You really think it's a bomb?" asked Ryan.

"If it's a bomb," the officer said, "it should have gone off by now. No," he added, "I don't think it's a bomb. We figure she's swiping something and hiding it away. Maybe she comes back and gets it. But we'll find out for sure tonight."

This was true. The arresting officer was on the phone next morning. The whole business had gone as planned, he told Ryan. A detachment of police had been assigned to cover the area. As they watched from the concealment of trees and shrubbery, the Bomber appeared with her small package. The police caught her red-handed and hustled her away to the station house. There was only one thing wrong. The package didn't have a bomb in it. It had no jewelry, diamonds or loot of any kind. All it held was table scraps.

"Well, that's a load off your mind," Ryan said sympathetically.

"That's what you think," said the officer. "The Bomber isn't a bomber or a crook or anything like that. She sings soprano. At the Metropolitan Opera," he added ruefully. "She's Frieda Hempel."

"How many of you," Ryan asked, "does she plan to sue for false arrest?"

"Nobody," the officer said. "She's a good sport. I never met a soprano before, but Frieda Hempel's OK. She wants to talk to somebody at the Society. She's coming to see you."

"I don't know a damned thing about opera," Ryan said.

"This doesn't have anything to do with opera," said the policeman. "It's about a dog."

Meeting an opera star for the first time, Ryan admitted to a certain amount of stage fright. But the soprano wasn't looking for applause or encores. She was looking, instead, for a small brown dog. It was only a mongrel stray, but Ryan realized that ancestry—human or animal—means nothing where affection is concerned.

As Miss Hempel explained, she had met the dog quite by accident in Central Park. The little stray had such an appeal for her that she would have taken the dog home immediately. But while the dog was friendly it was also shy. The animal would accept food but would always carry it away to a spot Miss Hempel had never been able to discover.

"Why do they think I am carrying a bomb all of a sudden?" she asked. "They should be used to seeing me in the park. I've been feeding my little dog there for the past five years!"

Rather than start another commotion in the police department, Miss Hempel was willing to adopt the dog formally. But before she could adopt it, she had to get hold of it.

"Miss Hempel," Ryan said, "opera's your business. Animals are mine. If you really want that dog, I'll have it here before the day's over."

Ryan drove to Central Park, carrying with him a wire cage with food in the bottom—and a fast-closing door. He found the dog easily enough in the spot Miss Hempel had described. For a time, Ryan began to wonder whether he hadn't made a rash promise to the opera star. The dog sniffed nervously at the cage, then dashed off, reappearing later for another look. Ryan waited patiently while the little animal circled the cage. Finally, the temptation grew too great. The stray ventured into the cage and Ryan sprung the door. He had acquired one dog for one soprano.

It took a week at the ASPCA shelter before the dog realized that civilization had something in its favor after all. When the opera star arrived to claim her prize, the dog's manners were as good as any penthouse-raised pet. The former stray made a triumphant exit in the arms of the soprano.

By way of apology, the police department sent Miss Hempel two dozen roses.

"They are beautiful," the opera star said, "but not so beautiful as my little dog."

20

The Cat's Meow

While the number of dogs in New York City shows signs of decreasing, Manhattan's cat population is on the rise. More New Yorkers keep cats than ever before. Apartment superintendents perhaps are more willing to tolerate a cat —and this is not overlooking the fact that it's a lot easier to smuggle in a contraband cat without a vigilant landlord being any the wiser. Another reason may be that city dwellers are beginning to realize that cats make ideal city pets. With living space at a premium in New York, most residents count themselves lucky to discover even a tiny apartment; two or three rooms and a foyer inspire New Yorkers with a giddy sense of endless vistas. A good-sized dog can take up a lot of this space without any difficulty at all, and still plead to be taken out for a nightly run. A cat can figure out ways to make himself comfortable almost anywhere, and believes in the principle of infinite riches in a little room.

Economic and logistic considerations aside, it would be pleasant to believe that another factor operates in the growth of the cat's popularity: that more people are starting to like cats purely because of the cat's own remarkable qualities of affection combined with independence, gracefulness, intelligence—and the ability generally to stay one up on the human he deigns to live with. People with touchy egos can be driven to despair by a cat's insistence on occasional periods of privacy and time for contemplation and meditation. The owner who prefers wildly enthusiastic tail-wagging to subtler and perhaps more intense demonstrations of love may develop the nagging impression that his cat doesn't have a very high opinion of him.

But these are childish reactions. It may be that we are starting to enjoy cats more because we are growing a little more mature, a little wiser. In any case, cats have patience enough to wait for us to catch up to them.

In the United States, cats number between 21 and 28 million (dogs, 22 to 26 million), with about 1.9 cats per family. Some experts have also suggested that for every cat with a home there's a cat making its way on its own. No one knows for sure exactly how many cats live specifically in New York; even Ryan himself prefers not to venture a guess. At any one time, the Society may house a little better than 250 cats as guests in its shelters. Within a year, it receives almost 13,000 cats for home adoption and collects more than 10,000 lost, abandoned or stray felines. Total number of cats handled in a year goes above 81,000.

The Society's hospital services examine and treat more than 5,000 cats each year. (Private veterinarians, taken altogether, see a much greater number.)

At best, however, these are only small clues to New York's sizable cat population. Cats aren't prone to giving out census information, and statistics are hard to come by. The number of dogs is easier to estimate because of licensing requirements. Cats, in New York, don't have to worry about such details.

Throughout the country, the question of cat licenses continues to come up now and again. Most legislators have wisely decided that cats are something special, that cats have been blithely ignoring the rather limited human concepts of ownership for about five thousand years and might just as well continue to do so.

Cats, say some of the lawmakers, just won't admit to being

owned by anybody. A dog, most often, will answer to his name or come when his owner calls, thereby establishing some rationale of ownership. A cat, subjected to the same test, will as likely as not choose to ignore the whole business, depending on what mood he's in. Thus, ownership in the narrowest legal sense becomes a little shaky where a cat is concerned. Lawyers have reached this conclusion after many years of careful investigation and deliberation. Any cat-owner could have told them that immediately.

In a way, the Society is relieved that cats don't have to wear licenses—on a humanitarian, rather than legal, basis. A cat obliged to wear a collar (to carry, in turn, a license) can get into an awful lot of trouble, such as catching himself on any kind of projection or finding a dozen other ways to become entangled.

Although unlicensed, cats still enjoy every protection of the anti-cruelty laws and every facility of the Society. They need it, no less than dogs. Ryan, and most other cat experts, believe that city owners should keep their cats indoors, but the cats themselves don't all agree with this and the New York jungle is as fascinating as the regular kind for these miniature tigers. Uncomfortably and, sometimes, fatally so.

Cats are ingenious, inventive, curious, imaginative, and in New York they demonstrate this by getting themselves into an implausible and colorful spectrum of difficulties. Ryan, who began as a specialist in horses and later moved to other, more unusual animals, has also spent a good part of his time rescuing cats.

"Usually," Ryan says, "you can get an animal out of trouble pretty fast. With cats, it can take one hell of a while."

Nothing involving a cat is really easy. But one thing Ryan has learned to cope with quickly is the classic situation of a frightened cat up a tree. Cats, as part of their inheritance, are expert tree climbers and have been since the first cat stepped out of the Ark. As silent, stalking hunters their ancestors were equally at home in the trees and on the ground. The twentieth-century cat remains, deep in his heart, a competent woodsman. By all rights, he should be able to climb a tree as well as his distant forebears.

Basically, he is able to do it. But as the well-known New York veterinarian Dr. Louis J. Camuti points out, a cat's claws curve *forward*. A cat has no problem climbing up something—but he has to climb down backwards. A young cat (and even a veteran) can suddenly turn panicky in the midst of this tricky operation, decide to stay where he is and broadcast to the world that he doesn't like it. The cat's panic in this situation is rivaled only by the owner's.

Complete fire departments, including rescue nets, hook and ladder, have been called to the rescue. The commotion often terrifies the cat still more. Ryan prefers the quieter approach. He uses a light, padded pole, something like the one grocers once employed to reach merchandise on a high shelf. This usually works quickly and effectively and does no harm to the cat except, perhaps, to offend his dignity. And, of course, there is always the chance that by the time Ryan reaches the scene the cat has figured out his own way of getting down.

Other urban snares are not so simple. Cats discover ways of infiltrating sewers, drainpipes, inaccessible stairwells. They appear on ledges of high-rise apartments and office buildings, behind newly constructed walls. In many of these situations it would appear theoretically impossible for any animal to find its way there. But cats manage to do it. Like Santa Claus, cats are also partial to chimneys.

Cats do land on their feet after a fall and have been known to survive a drop of several stories. On the other hand, a drop of only a few feet may sometimes result in a broken neck or fractured spine. Ryan once answered a midnight call from a woman whose pet had tumbled into a narrow, slotlike area between two buildings. Against all advice to cat-owners to keep their windows screened, the owner had left hers open. The cat, naturally, decided to explore the window ledge and a moment later found himself at the bottom of the areaway, two stories below.

Training his spotlight on the animal, Ryan judged the cat had suffered no damage. The tabby crouched on the cement far below, looking as tiny as a fly at the bottom of a well.

Ryan's first thought was to get closer to the cat. "How about the people in the downstairs apartment?" he asked. "Will they let me go fishing out their window?"

The woman went to investigate, found the apartment locked and no one at home. The stores and offices in the opposite building were shut.

Ryan, who always carries a lasso with him, rigged up a fast-slipping knot and gained the required length by adding clothesline. While the woman held his spotlight, Ryan leaned out the window. Like a deep-sea fisherman, he dropped his line over the side and slowly payed it out toward the cat.

Below, the tabby eyed the approach of the cord. When it reached the bottom, the cat stood on his hind legs and batted it back and forth, as if Ryan had invented a new game.

The woman was on the verge of tears; but the cat simply was not taking the business seriously.

Ryan made a few more passes with the lasso. His aim was to drop the loop over the cat's shoulders and front paws; he did not dare rope the animal's head, for the noose would strangle the cat or break his neck before Ryan had a chance to hoist him very far.

Ryan wanted the cat to step through the loop and he became rapidly convinced that the cat had no intention of doing so. From his arsenal of rescue equipment, Ryan took a bottle of sardine oil, soaked a bit of cloth with it and lowered the bait directly in front of the loop.

The cat shied away to a corner.

"Oh, I forgot to tell you," said the woman. "He hates fish."

Ryan sighed and retrieved his lure. "What do you feed him?" Ryan asked.

The woman told him that the cat usually ate table scraps and, occasionally, canned dog food. She opened a can and Ryan prepared his bait again.

This time, instead of stepping through the loop, the cat merely walked around to the other side and attacked the bait from the rear. Ryan hastily pulled it up again. On the following attempt, he dangled the food in such a way that the cat would be obliged to step through the loop.

The cat decided he wasn't particularly hungry.

Ryan wiped his perspiring forehead and suggested changing the bait.

"He loves ham sandwiches," said the woman. "He's always begging whenever I eat one."

"We don't need to try a whole sandwich," Ryan said. "Just the ham."

Even with this new temptation, Ryan's luck did not improve. "Lady," he said, "isn't there something he *really* likes?"

"Well," said the owner, "I suppose the best treat for him is chicken."

"Good," said Ryan. "Let's send down some chicken."

"I don't have any," the woman said. "I mean, I have some chicken but it isn't cooked."

"Cook it," said Ryan.

The woman hurriedly set a pan on the stove. "He enjoys it Southern Fried," she said.

"I don't care if it's chicken *cacciatore*," Ryan said. "You make it the way he likes it."

In a little while, the scent of cooking filled the apartment. Ryan had to admit that even though the woman was careless about her windows, she was a better-than-average cook.

The chicken smelled delicious. At this hour of the morning, Ryan himself would have been willing to step into a lasso for some of it.

The woman handed him a drumstick. Ryan let it cool for a moment, then hopefully lowered it to the cat.

Without hesitation, the cat leaped for the bait. In a flash, Ryan tightened up on the lasso. A few seconds later, the cat appeared at the window and Ryan hauled him safely over the side.

The cat still held the drumstick in his mouth.

"Might as well let him eat the rest," Ryan said. "He deserves it."

The woman fussed and crooned over the little tabby. The cat calmly continued eating the drumstick, as if frantic humans and midnight rescues were only a trivial aspect of his day and, at worst, a minor inconvenience.

Ryan packed up his gear and left the apartment. Knowing cats, Ryan could not shake off the haunting suspicion that the little tabby might have engineered the whole affair on purpose. Cats generally end up getting what they want, through methods often complex and devious. As Sir Walter Scott told Washington Irving:

"Cats are a mysterious kind of folk. There is more passing in their minds than we are aware of!"

21

Airport Ark

In addition to the animals Ryan and other ASPCA agents hoist out of chimneys and rescue from skyscraper ledges, the Society cares for still another group: animals traveling by air.

On the Society's 1¼-acre site in the middle of Idlewild's Air Cargo Center, a herd of cows may graze peacefully one day, replaced, the next, by trumpeting elephants. A jet plane from Africa unloads a zebra looking as if it hadn't had time to change out of striped pajamas. Several hundred monkeys and 10,000 baby chicks unexpectedly show up for dinner, along with pandas, pangolins and polar bears. From Paris, London, Berlin, Tokyo, 175,000 animals so far—110 different species—have found rest, refreshment and shelter at the Society's Sidney H. Coleman Animalport. Built in 1958 at a cost of $300,000, the shelter combines (from an animal's viewpoint) the best features of the Waldorf-Astoria and Sun Valley—with the Mayo Clinic attached. For completeness of equipment, facilities, services and personal care, no other air terminal in the Western Hemisphere has anything to match the Animalport.

Of all animals entering the United States from abroad, 80 percent arrive by air. Before the Animalport existed, the airlines people had to cope with live cargo themselves. The phrase "more fun than a barrel of monkeys" rings bitterly in the ears of men trying to run a busy airport. Once, a band of apes—obviously clever and well disciplined—made a break for freedom. In the course of the mutiny, they swarmed all over the control tower, as if they had determined to capture this strategic position first.

In a bold encircling movement the control tower staff, reinforced by a division of cargo handlers, eventually got the apes back into the cages. Fortunately, the simians had not yet taken over the communications system; otherwise, pilots requesting landing instructions might still be circling Idlewild.

Elephants have wandered out onto the runway; so have horses. From pre-Animalport days, the story goes that a terminal official on hand to welcome a visiting diplomat noticed something peculiar about the crowd of journalists and photographers milling at the gate. The manager turned to his assistant.

"*That's* a reporter?" he asked, pointing at a large chimpanzee amid the newsmen.

The chimp's coverage might have been no less intelligible than the reportage in some newspaper columns, but not being accredited, he was nabbed and led back to his own quarters.

Despite the facetious aspects, handling live cargo gave the airlines a serious headache. Baggage clerks, for example, don't really know what to do about lions; the learning process in this instance could be painful and possibly fatal. Not only might the humans be hurt, improper handling might injure the animals. Since the airlines had no proper means of caring for live shipments, the animals were, at best, uncomfortable and often neglected through sheer inadequacy of facilities. Delayed en route, animals went hungry, thirsty, overlooked or lost in the shuffle.

With the stream of airborne animals growing bigger every day, the Society took one of the most imaginative steps in the history of the American humane movement. Hugh Paine, the Society's President at that time, and the late Warren McSpadden, General Manager of the ASPCA, laid the groundwork for the project. The expense of building and operating an adequate shelter at Idlewild would be enormous. But there was no question in anyone's mind that the animals needed help urgently. Airline officials welcomed the Society's proposal and the ASPCA swung into planning sessions for one of the most extensive and specialized installations it had ever undertaken.

In Britain, the Royal Society for the Prevention of Cruelty to Animals had, in 1952, opened the world's first shelter for animal air travelers. Arthur L. Amundsen, the Society's present Director of Operations, flew to England to gain firsthand know-how about running a shelter of this type. He also spent months in half a dozen European countries, studying their methods of air cargo handling.

"We had everything to learn," Amundsen says. "The decision to build the Animalport had already been made, though at that point we didn't know much about feeding, health regulations and all the rest. We learned fast. We had to!"

The shelter the Society envisioned would cost better than a quarter of a million dollars (it came out, at the end, costing $500,000 more). Architects and builders started work. Within only 18 months, Animalport opened to guests.

Aside from planning for the health and comfort of just about every species of animal in the world, one of the knottiest problems was what to name the shelter. In the Society's opinion, "hostel" sounded too British. In a burst of inspiration, the ASPCA's Mrs. George Fielding Eliot came up with "Animalport."

By any name, the Animalport would be a blessing. "The ASPCA is fulfilling its purpose in providing an animal traveler's aid society," says Dr. Leonard Goss, director of the Cleveland Zoo. The assistant cargo supervisor for one of the big airlines adds, "There's simply no comparison today with what it used to be around here. The Animalport's taken the worry and bother off our shoulders and, believe me, there used to be plenty!" Every zoo curator and livestock dealer whose shipments have benefited from Animalport services feels the same way.

The Animalport overlooks nothing that any animal could possibly want. First, in pure logistics, the two-story sun-tan brick building was planned in the most minute detail. The indoor loading area accommodates the biggest trucks that might ever bring in shipments. All gates stay locked until completion of unloading. Because the Animalport stands in the center of Idlewild's cargo area, animals reach the shelter without delay or overexposure to bad weather—an advantage a human traveler might think about wistfully. The Animalport's 5,000 square feet include 60 kennels and cages with attached exercise runs for cats, dogs and smaller animals. Twelve box stalls, available for horses, have been so devised that when the Animalport has something really large and weighty, such as several elephants, they can be immediately converted to match the guests' requirements. After each occupant—gorilla, cheetah or what have you—leaves to catch its plane, Society workers armed with steam-hoses, scrubbing brushes and disinfectant prepare for the next arrival; like everything about the Animalport, the quarters sparkle. The only creatures the Society doesn't welcome are germs.

Medically, the Animalport is equipped to give animal patients everything from a vitamin pill to major surgery in the $8,000 ultramodern veterinary clinic. Specially trained members of the Veterinary Medical Association of New York City take charge of diagnosis and treatment and perform any needed operations. Like humans, animals don't choose convenient times to be sick; the clinic works a 24-hour schedule and, day or night, can go on an emergency basis instantly. A special isolation ward houses animals stricken by contagious illnesses.

Polar bears don't enjoy the same temperature as macaws

from the jungle. The Animalport has foreseen this, and the building is entirely climate-conditioned, with individual controls. One area can be made to feel like the North Pole; the one next to it, the Belgian Congo. Animalport workers may become geographically confused, stepping from the arctic to the equator, but the animals stay healthy, cheerful and comfortable.

These external comforts make up only part of the story. The Animalport cares for the inner animal, too, and the guests are fussier and more demanding about their food than the clientele of any luxury hotel or restaurant. The commissary and frozen-food department stock exotic items Escoffier never heard of. Chefs in the diet kitchen offer a menu which no maître d'hôtel could hope to approach. It might, in part, read like this:

NECTAR AND HONEY

(Special for hummingbirds)

ORCHIDS

(Squirrel monkeys' favorite)

AFRICAN FENNEC FOX PLATTER

Meal Worms   **Raisins**   **Baby Food**   **Rolled Oats**

ASSORTED FRUITS

(For simian patrons)

Apples   Bananas   Oranges

HORSE MEAT AU NATUREL

(The delight of lions, tigers, ocelots and eagles)

VEGETARIAN SPECIALS

(For horses, cows, elephants)

Assorted Hay and Grains   Fresh Greens

BEVERAGES

Milk, Fresh or Powdered   Orange Juice   Fresh Water

The above only hints at the variety of food served routinely at the Animalport, from bamboo shoots to more commonplace entries such as dog food, dog biscuits, oleo, frozen fish, birdseed. Individual guests often have their own eccentric tastes. One famous racehorse preferred artichokes. The Animalport had none on hand at the moment, but got them for him in a hurry.

Food, facilities and attention like this, combined with incredibly modest fees, would make for fame anywhere. Livestock breeders, explorers, zookeepers and air transport companies all over the world have learned about the shelter.

The first guest was a cat from Paris. During that opening year, the Animalport played host to 21,700 more animals. The number rose 31 percent the following year, to reach 28,500; to 33,000 in 1960; to 55,297 in 1961; and in 1962 to 69,605—without a sign of decrease in the future.

Monkeys make up the biggest single group, with over 22,000 so far; tropical birds come next, totaling 12,000 to date. One-of-a-kind animals have included a full-grown polar bear and a pangolin, a type of Malayan anteater. In between come numbers of snow leopards, gorillas, aardvarks, sea lions, walruses, foxes, skunks, lions, tigers, lizards, chinchillas. Most recent visitors have been a phalanger, or Australian flying squirrel; and a *Rana goliath,* a giant frog six feet long—spectacular but, in some opinions, not as handsome as an ordinary bullfrog.

Running a shelter for guests of these diverse sizes and temperaments demands, among other things, the versatility of a hotelkeeper and the organizing ability of a field marshal; perpetual optimism; a grasp of psychology (animal and human); a fairly high degree of immunity to shock; and, of course, an abiding love for animals no matter how rambunctious they may become—which is often very much so.

The man with these qualifications is George F. Bauer, the Animalport's Resident Manager. The fifty-five-year-old Bauer's friendly smile comes from a naturally warm and outgoing disposition, and the wisdom to know that sometimes the best thing to do is just keep smiling.

Manhattan-born Bauer took pre-med courses at Cornell

University for three years, decided he didn't really want to be a doctor and quit to join the New York Police. After two years on the force, he transferred to the Mounted Division and served in it for the next eighteen years. He retired in 1956 and joined the Society as an agent. When the Animalport opened, the Society chose Bauer as the ideal man for the job.

Since then, Bauer has drawn on all his capabilities—including some he didn't even realize he possessed. Every animal presents a different problem and, considering the thousands of creatures passing through the Animalport, this is enough to test anybody's ingenuity.

With simians making up the largest single group of visitors, Bauer has plenty of opportunities to match wits with them. The primates can be most appealing. Baby gorillas, for example, crave affection, love to be held and fussed over. But, like children, the simians change from angels to fiends in a split second. The mischief they find is beyond prediction.

One chimpanzee discovered how to unhook his crate clasp. Delighted with this new knowledge, the chimp climbed out and ducked through a window to a food chest. He also challenged Bauer to a wrestling match. Instead of accepting, the quick-thinking manager seized a banana and lured the animal into a nearby cage. Afterwards, Bauer installed chimpanzee-proof window locks.

The Animalport makes a practice of opening the guests' crates as soon after arrival as possible, to give the animals food and water and let them stretch their legs. Twenty-five South American monkeys took advantage of this operation one day. Before anyone knew what was going on, all twenty-five decided to take an unguided tour of the Animalport. They streamed out, dashed en masse into one of the stable rooms and climbed up into the girders. It took Bauer and his assistants six hours to collect them.

A young gorilla didn't take kindly to a veterinarian's attempt to give him an injection. Bauer and two staff members held the gorilla firmly on the operating table, but as soon as the vet approached with a hypodermic the patient tossed his keepers in every direction. One man went bulleting through the door, the vet ended up in a corner, another helper came to rest in the sink. For a moment, it looked as though the gorilla was going to take over the job of running the Animalport. He finally calmed down, resigned his temporary position and strode back to his cage.

Two other gorillas acted as if they wanted to be maintenance men at the Animalport. En route to Kobe, Japan, via California, the 400-pound visitors had arrived at the Animalport in cases strewn with banana leaves. Californians don't blink at exotic visitors, but state law strictly prohibits introduction of foreign vegetation. This includes African banana leaves, and Bauer's biggest job was cleaning the cases. He and his assistants began raking busily—until the gorillas grabbed the rakes out of their hands.

Bauer wouldn't have minded if the big fellows had done any work with the implements, but the gorillas merely sat there, cradling the rakes in their arms. You just don't take things from gorillas unless they feel like giving them up. The gorillas relinquished the rakes, to seize them again a few minutes later. This went on for most of the night and it was only toward the small hours of the morning that the last leaf was raked away. Government inspectors complimented the weary Bauer on his thoroughness and California was saved from banana leaves.

Gorillas, as Bauer well knows, have their childish moments. Dr. Keets Pickett, noted authority on wild animals, recognizes this too and goes so far as to dress his young gorillas in children's clothes. The animals, completely outfitted in diapers, jackets and caps, sit with Dr. Pickett in the passenger area. Bauer had two of Dr. Pickett's traveling companions at the Animalport one day and carried them to the waiting airship.

"Here," Bauer said, handing over the fully dressed gorillas, "I've brought your pilot and co-pilot."

From what Bauer has seen of gorillas, the airline was lucky that the animals didn't take his remarks seriously. It would have been an interesting flight.

Ninety percent of the dogs arriving at the Animalport from Europe belong to GI's. One armored unit, being transferred to the United States, sent a lion.

The unit had adopted the animal as a mascot when it was a cub. Now it weighed 275 pounds and the soldiers decided that their pet would bring them better luck if he were honorably discharged from the service and retired to a zoo. Accordingly, they shipped the lion to the Animalport and detached two sergeants as keepers.

The lion showed up first, looking hungry and thirsty. Bauer fed and watered the mascot and released it into one of the Animalport cages. When the sergeants finally appeared, they were a little disturbed at this. They appreciated Bauer's care, but there was one hitch.

"The way we get him to go back into his cage," one of the sergeants said, "is to put some meat in it. If he's already eaten, he isn't going to be interested."

Bauer faced the possibility of waiting until the lion developed a new appetite. In the meantime, bursting with energy and high spirits, the lion had bitten off a water tap in the cage. The sergeants agreed it might be wiser to get the lion into his traveling case at the earliest opportunity.

"He's really very friendly," the sergeant assured Bauer. "I don't think we'll have any trouble."

Using the direct approach, the three men entered the cage, surrounded the unsuspecting lion and shoved it into the traveling box.

"What did I tell you?" said the sergeant. "He's just like a big puppy. He loves to jump up on you, too."

"I'm glad," Bauer said, "you didn't mention that before."

Bauer was relieved that the transfer went so smoothly. There had been only one uneasy moment. It had taken place before the sergeants' arrival, when the lion, turning frisky, began roaring and racing back and forth in the cage.

Bauer, at that point, ducked out of the room and held the door tightly shut. His wife, passing by just then, stopped to see what the trouble was.

"We've got a lion in there," Bauer said.

"You don't need to tell me," his wife observed. Then she began to scream.

"If you're scared," Bauer told her, "stay away from the cage."

"I can't," she said. "You're standing on my foot."

"Expect the unexpected" is George Bauer's motto. It is an easy one to follow because the unexpected happens so often. Since there is no set schedule for arrivals, Bauer can't guess what each new day will bring. Even when people try to alert him ahead of time, it doesn't always work out. One shipper telephoned Bauer that 90 head of cattle, bound for Turkey, would arrive at the Animalport in groups of 30 during the following three days.

The appreciative Bauer thanked him for the information. For once, Bauer thought, he would have time to prepare calmly for his guests. Two minutes after putting down the phone, Bauer looked out the window and saw a large cattle van roll into the loading area.

The truckers had made better time than estimated. Stretching far down the road were other vans, holding the entire consignment of 90 cows and bulls, all waiting for accommodations.

Until four A.M., Bauer and his staff tore out partitions to

convert horse stalls into cattle pens. Even then, the cattle-lift didn't go as planned. Shortage of cargo space prevented the airlines from flying out the whole shipment and Bauer was left in charge of 12 bulls. They stayed at the Animalport five weeks until the company brought in 14 more heifers to make up a full load.

During the waiting period, Idlewild workers dubbed the livestock "Bauer's Herd." Each morning, Bauer would drive his charges into an outdoor enclosure and bring them back again at dusk.

"The airport people got a big kick out of that," Bauer says. "They liked the idea of cattle browsing around. It made Idlewild look so restful."

Along with expecting the unexpected goes Bauer's talent for improvising. When four enormous sea lions, traveling from California to Hamburg, Germany, were grounded be-cause of a shipping error, Bauer offered to take them. Only after his invitation was gratefully accepted did Bauer realize he had never dealt with sea lions in his life.

Undaunted, Bauer proved his ingenuity by packing huge blocks of ice around the sea lions' cases and installing a shower nozzle to spray cold water. For the animals' menu, Bauer provided smelts. The sea lions stayed eight days. From their joyous yelps and enthusiastic applause, Bauer assumed they enjoyed every minute of it.

When cargo handlers walked off the job, refusing (under-standably) to unload a pair of Bengal tigers, Bauer under-took the job. The problem was to transfer the tigers from one set of traveling cases to another. Using two-by-fours, Bauer and his men rigged up a sturdy passageway between the two containers. As a further precaution, Bauer parked a truck behind the new cases, where it functioned as a back-stop.

"Tigers come out fast," Bauer says. "They have enough push to knock the whole business apart."

Had that happened, Bauer would have been confronted with two tigers on the loose. Fortunately, he wasn't called on to solve this problem, but he undoubtedly would have thought of something.

Bauer has to use as much imagination in dealing with humans as he does with animals. Many of the owners and keepers don't speak English. Usually, he can find an interpreter among all the nations represented at Idlewild. A Hindu elephant boy nearly stumped him, but Bauer telephoned Air India and was able to carry on a three-way conversation. First, Bauer told the Air India people what he wanted to tell the mahout; the mahout would listen to the translation, tell Air India what *he* had to say, hand the receiver back to Bauer, who would take over again. The system didn't match the UN's simultaneous translations, but it worked. It turned out that, among other things, the mahout wanted a haircut.

The mahout was also disturbed because his elephant wouldn't eat. Elephant-tending is an honored profession in India, handed down from father to son, and a sick animal would have ruined the mahout's reputation at home—especially since the elephant was a gift from the children of India to the children of America.

Despite his skill, the mahout could discover no way to perk up his valuable charge. Bauer finally called the Bronx Zoo, whose curator recommended bread and carrots. The diet worked well, although Bauer was surely pegged for a very odd shopper at the supermarket, where he went in search of extra provisions.

There, Bauer loaded his cart with bread—twenty loaves of it. At the checking station, the startled clerk shook his head. "Mister," he said, "that must be one big turkey you're going to stuff."

"I'm not going to stuff a turkey," Bauer answered, "I'm going to stuff an elephant."

If the supermarket clerk considered Bauer a nut, one druggist thought him a downright fraud. Resident Manager means just what it says: Bauer and his wife live in a charming four-room apartment on the second floor of the Animalport. This is difficult for some people to believe, as Bauer learned when his wife developed a cough during an auto trip through Florida.

Bauer stopped to buy a codeine compound. He signed the narcotics book, paid for his purchase and started out the door. The druggist raced after him.

"Hey!" he shouted. "What are you trying to pull? What kind of a phony address is this? Idlewild International Airport! Nobody lives on an airport!"

"I do," Bauer said.

He showed the man his business card. After much explanation, Bauer was allowed to leave with the medicine. He still has the impression the druggist wasn't quite convinced.

The airport residence does have another slight disadvantage. Mrs. Bauer has to drive ten miles to reach the nearest shopping center; and while she has plenty of neighbors—20,000 Idlewild employees—she can't pop next door to borrow a cup of sugar. On the other hand, she can always find a bunch of bananas or a bushel of orchids. Nevertheless, living at the Animalport helps Bauer give his charges the constant attention they require.

Animalport guests have included Iron Liege, the Kentucky Derby winner; Jamin, the French trotter; Ribald, an Italian stud horse insured for $6,000,000. Bauer has looked after animals belonging to celebrities such as the late Aly Khan, Elizabeth Arden, Arthur Godfrey and Victor Borge. But an owner's fame doesn't figure in Animalport operations. The animal comes first; Bauer and the Animalport staff are as attentive to the needs of a lonely kitten as they are to the welfare of a million-dollar thoroughbred.

One of the airlines attaches a special red-and-white label to all its animal crates, whether they hold prickly porcupines, leopards or baby monkeys. It reads, HANDLE WITH LOVE.

The Society's Animalport takes this advice to heart.

22

The Scent of Friendship

"Handle with love" may be another clue to Ryan's secret for getting along with animals. Some people swear he carries a supply of tranquilizers up his sleeve. Others disregard the tranquilizer theory and insist that he mutters some kind of Irish spell. Ryan does neither. Tranquilizers might conceivably come in handy in rescue work (more for the human than the animal) but Ryan has never felt the need for them. Of Irish spells he knows nothing, although he occasionally wishes he did. They would make life a lot easier.

A more scientific explanation might be that Ryan doesn't give off a fear-scent. Some authorities believe that when a human being is scared and his adrenalin and other glands start working faster, he emits an unmistakable scent which animals detect immediately. This could be part of Ryan's secret—but not all of it. No human being is totally fearless and Ryan admits that sometimes he has had the pants scared off him.

There is a simpler and perhaps unprovable possibility. If animals recognize the scent of fear, it might be plausible to wonder whether they also recognize another scent: the scent of friendship. Ryan cares deeply about animals and this attitude may well show up in subtle movements, tone of voice, gestures and general attitude. Humans, often unconsciously, respond to a similar quality in other humans. Animals, being closer to nature, with keener instincts and intuitions, may be even more alert to it.

Whatever the secret, or combination of secrets, it works. But a few who have seen it work still don't believe it. A couple of years ago, answering a call from a restaurant in the East Sixties, Ryan found a police car parked in front and two policemen standing uneasily a few feet away. Ryan recognized one of the men, but something peculiar caught his attention. The policeman's cap had no visor.

Ryan pulled up beside him. "Is that the new uniform?" he asked.

"Don't get smart, Ryan," said the officer. "I'm lucky I still got my head on." He gestured toward the squad car. On the back seat, holding the policeman's visor between his paws and gnawing away happily, crouched a dog about the size of a timber wolf.

The policeman explained that the dog appeared out of nowhere and sauntered into the restaurant. Most of the diners then departed hastily, many of them forgetting to leave tips. A waiter volunteered to usher the dog out. However, as the situation developed, the waiter decided it was safer to set the dog a good example by running out of the restaurant first. The dog followed and was on the verge of catching up when the police car happened along.

"What else could I do?" the officer told Ryan. "I opened the back door and he jumped in. When I turned around to take another look at him, he bit off my hat."

"So what's the problem?" asked Ryan.

"The problem is I don't like back-seat drivers. Not when they think I'm Little Red Riding Hood."

"Oh, is that all?" said Ryan. "Why didn't you tell me that in the first place?"

The ASPCA agent pulled his car even with the officer's and opened his own back door. He went to the squad car and opened its door. "Come on, fellow," he called. "Good boy!"

The big dog jumped unhestitatingly into Ryan's vehicle. The policemen stared, openmouthed.

"Listen, Ryan," one of them said at last. "Tell me the truth. You set this whole thing up, didn't you? I mean . . . you knew all about it, or this is your dog or something. . . ."

"I swear," Ryan shook his head, "I never saw him before in my life."

"Then you slipped him a needle . . . a pill . . ."

"Never," Ryan insisted. "You just have to know how to talk to a dog."

"Good boy!" snorted the policeman. "Good doggie! I can say that too. So look what happens."

"It's personality," said Ryan. "Some people have it, some people don't." He put the car in gear and waved at the policemen. "Let me know whenever I can help you out."

In the back seat, the dog still gnawed on the visor. Ryan wondered whether to take it away, but the dog seemed to be enjoying it so much he decided not to push his luck. Sometimes, letting sleeping dogs lie is not a bad policy; it may also apply to dogs who have taken a fancy to police department caps.

Not long afterwards, Ryan helped out the police force again. At two o'clock in the morning, he met the officers in the hallway of a cheap roominghouse. There a man sprawled face down on the floor while a snarling dog stood guard. Ryan asked whether the man was alive or dead.

"How can we tell?" a policeman answered. "The dog won't let us go near him."

This time, Ryan's powers of persuasion didn't work. The dog's loyalty was to his master. Even an offer of food did not shake it.

Ryan finally lassoed the dog and improvised a muzzle from a length of cord.

"He's dead, all right," said one of the policemen. "Dead drunk, that is!"

The officers set about reviving the merrymaker. At Ryan's side, the dog strained at the leash and whimpered.

At last, the man sat up and rubbed his eyes. "OK, mister," an officer told him. "Party's over. Round up your dog and get to bed."

The man blinked. "What dog?"

"What dog!" cried the policeman. "Your pal here. He's been looking after you for the past hour. Don't tell me you got so loaded you don't even remember your own dog."

"Not my dog," the man muttered. "Never saw him before."

At the sound of the man's voice, the dog tried to leap forward. He wagged his tail and pawed at the air.

"Well, he's sure seen *you* before," Ryan said.

The man got shakily to his feet and made an attempt to brush off his shabby coat. "Not my dog," he repeated. "Just let me alone. I made enough of a fool of myself already."

The landlady, who had been watching the proceedings from the foot of the stairs, raised her voice. "You don't need to tell us. Hooting, hollering, carrying on for half the night. You ought to be ashamed of yourself."

The man did not answer. Ryan stepped over to the landlady. "Listen," he said, "what's wrong with this guy? That dog belongs to him. Who's he trying to kid?"

"Sure it's his dog," said the woman. "You think I don't know who lives here—two-footed *or* four-footed?"

Once again Ryan offered the dog to the owner, who still refused. The ASPCA agent had no choice but to take the animal to the shelter. Throughout the ride, the dog howled and whined pitifully. But even when Ryan had walked out

of the roominghouse door, the man had made no attempt
to follow.

Late next morning, Ryan happened to be in the adoption
office when a familiar figure entered. It was the owner, looking gray and ill shaven, but considerably improved from the
time Ryan had seen him last.

The man walked briskly to the desk. "I believe you people have my dog here."

"What!" Ryan exploded. "At three o'clock this morning
you didn't have a dog. You didn't even have a puppy."

"My dog is here," the man said firmly. "I want him back."

"Mister," Ryan said, "you can have any dog you want.
Just tell me one thing. Why didn't you make up your mind
before? You knew damned well it was your dog; and I knew
damned well it was your dog. Why didn't you save yourself
a lot of time and trouble?"

The man drew closer to Ryan and lowered his voice.
"That dog's the best friend I got in the world. He'd give up
his life for me if he had to. And I guess I'd do the same for
him. But there's something else," he added sheepishly. "I
go off the reservation sometimes. Once in a while maybe I
drink too much. You got to understand this. I respect that
dog and I don't want nobody thinking he runs in bad company. So what else am I gonna do? What kind of a reputation would a dog get, hanging around an old drunk? Sure
I let on he wasn't mine. I didn't want to embarrass him."

While embarrassing a dog might represent mental cruelty,
trying to make one swim a good part of the length of the
Hudson River falls in a different category. Ryan was ordered near Poughkeepsie one day on a complaint by an elderly German, a retired merchant seaman named Schimmel.
Mr. Schimmel operated a boathouse and from his dock had
observed several men on the deck of a small yacht. Paddling
valiantly alongside was a shepherd dog. The men told Mr.

Schimmel they had been on the water two days, en route to New York City. They planned to continue their trip by yacht; the dog, by swimming.

Ryan had investigated dog fighting and dog racing. Dog swimming was new to him. Anyone who would consider swimming a dog down the Hudson must, in Ryan's opinion, be out of his head. He wondered whether Mr. Schimmel had misunderstood. In Poughkeepsie, Ryan discovered that the facts were as Mr. Schimmel had reported. What Mr. Schimmel had not mentioned was that the gentlemen involved were advertising people from one of the Manhattan agencies.

Ryan found the yacht tied up near Schimmel's boathouse. Bobbing up and down on a float tied alongside was the dog, looking fairly well tuckered out. Ryan hailed the craft and a man in a blue blazer and yachting cap appeared on deck. He beckoned Ryan to come up, and pumped his hand warmly.

"I'm Buzz Smalley, from Clapper, Crowder and Dun," he said. "Glad to have you aboard, sir. This is one time it makes sense to say that, eh?" Mr. Smalley grinned cheerfully. "Did the shop send you up here?"

Ryan advised Mr. Smalley that he represented the ASPCA.

"Wonderful!" Mr. Smalley cried. "That makes it all the better. Now we can really get an official endorsement—"

"I didn't come up here to endorse—" Ryan began.

"That's really good thinking," Mr. Smalley hurried on. "Give the campaign a lot more sock. I can see it now." He sketched at the air with his hand. "Towser's Dog Biscuits! A bow-wow-wow! Enough pure dog-power in every box to let your dog swim the Hudson River! Then we cut to your testimonial—"

"Hey, wait a minute," Ryan said. "If you put that dog in

the water, the only testimonial you're going to get is a summons."

The grin disappeared from Mr. Smalley's face. "Listen, fellow," he said, "I don't think you understand. I'm talking about Towser's Dog Biscuits. *The* Towser's Dog Biscuits. That's one of CC&D's major clients."

"That may mean a lot to you," Ryan said, "but it doesn't mean a damned thing to me. I don't want that dog to swim another stroke."

The rest of the agency people had meanwhile gathered on the deck: a photographer, his assistant and a sallow young man who, as Ryan learned later, was the writer for the account. They all looked inquiringly at Mr. Smalley.

"We'll get this straightened out," the account executive muttered, "and we'll get it straightened out now." He strode down the little gangplank and headed for the row of boathouses.

Ten minutes later he was back. "I just talked to Fitz Crowder," he announced to his associates. "He says: go! That dog's full of pep, he wants to swim and, by God, he's going to swim."

"Not while I'm here," Ryan said.

So far, Ryan knew, the account executive had shown no real evidence of cruelty toward the dog. The animal still sat on the float and until Mr. Smalley actually forced the dog into the water, Ryan's hands were tied. He admitted this frankly to Mr. Smalley. "But," Ryan said, "don't think that's the end of it. I'm going to stay here. I'll be here every minute of the day. If you make one move—"

"You," said Mr. Smalley, "get the hell off this boat, before I have *you* arrested for . . . for piracy!"

Ryan shrugged and went ashore. He found Mr. Schimmel at the boathouse and told him the problem.

"That's all right," the merchant seaman said, "you stay with me. Long as you want. When you get tired watching,

I watch." He slapped Ryan on the shoulder. "Like at sea, eh? By Gott, they won't ruin a good dog like that."

Mr. Schimmel pulled an enormous pair of binoculars from his gear and handed them to Ryan. For the rest of the afternoon the two men waited in the boathouse, taking turns keeping an eye on the yacht.

At dusk, the assistant photographer hauled in the float and brought the dog aboard. Ryan saw little other activity on the yacht. There were lights in the cabin and once he caught sight of a face, Mr. Smalley's, peering briefly from a porthole. Later on, Mr. Schimmel shared some corned beef hash with the ASPCA agent.

The seaman offered to take the night watch. Ryan, without even removing his shoes, gratefully curled up under a tarpaulin. He had been napping only a couple of hours when Schimmel's voice roused him.

"Quick! Quick!" the seaman urged. "They're putting out!"

Ryan scrambled to his feet. The yacht had already gained the middle of the river. He stumbled through the boathouse to the little dock, where Schimmel had already begun to start the motor of a speedboat.

At first, the ASPCA agent feared Mr. Smalley would outrun Schimmel's own rickety craft; but the German cut the water with all power on, the motor protesting like a dull saw cutting cross-grain through a board. Ryan hung on with both hands while Mr. Schimmel executed a tight, neat arc and swung ahead of the yacht.

The yacht captain stopped his engines. The furious account executive appeared at the wheel. "Clear off, you idiot!" he shouted. "We're going to New Jersey. You've got no authority outside this state."

Ryan stood up in the bow of the speedboat. "Go right ahead," he called. "I'll phone the Jersey State Police—just to let 'em know you're on your way."

The account executive and the captain held a hurried conversation. Ryan could overhear nothing; but a few moments later the yacht put about and headed for the pier once more. Soaked to the skin, Ryan and Mr. Schimmel chugged back to the boathouse.

The night maneuvers must have exhausted the account executive. All next morning and afternoon, Ryan saw no sign of Mr. Smalley or his colleagues. The captain and mate disembarked once to bring on provisions. Ryan and Schimmel continued their turns with the binoculars.

The agent suspected that the yacht might try more evasive tactics; Schimmel agreed, and kept the speedboat ready. Ryan's guess was correct. About three in the morning, the yacht began to pull away again. Ryan and Schimmel overtook it without difficulty.

"Listen, Ryan," Mr. Smalley shouted down through cupped hands, "what will it cost to get you off my back?"

"It'll cost you whatever it takes to run that yacht down to New York," Ryan yelled, "and figure out another way to advertise dog biscuits."

Mr. Smalley shook his head. "The campaign," he said, drawing himself up, "will go on as planned!"

Nevertheless, the yacht turned and made for shore once again.

Ryan began to lose track of time during the next few days. Sometimes Mr. Smalley would keep the craft tied up for an entire day and night; the photographer's assistant would romp with the dog, the copywriter would lounge in the sun while the account executive paced back and forth.

Then, unpredictably, Mr. Smalley would again try to break out of harbor. But Ryan and the old seaman never abandoned their watch and were after the craft immediately, the speedboat buzzing like a ruptured hornet.

Throughout another four days and nights, Ryan lived in the boathouse, eating corned beef hash. Once in a while he managed to shave, although he never dared wash out all his clothes at the same time. The advertising men on the yacht had begun to look equally frazzled, despite several bottles of gin and vermouth recently shipped aboard.

Mr. Schimmel, by contrast, seemed to enjoy himself immensely. "We hold out a little longer," he cheerfully assured Ryan, "and they have a mutiny on that yacht."

Late in the morning of the sixth day, a long black car pulled up at the yacht slip. A stubby, gray-haired man in a tattersall vest and a tweed suit stepped out briskly and trotted up the gangplank. This, as Ryan found out later, was none other than Mr. Fitz Crowder in person. After a long conference on deck, Mr. Crowder and Mr. Smalley signaled Ryan to come aboard.

"I told you," Schimmel chuckled gleefully. "Now they want to parley."

On the yacht, Ryan explained again that this was a potentially cruel act against an animal and clearly against the law. To anyone with respect at all for an animal, it was also against plain common sense.

"Now, by Godfrey," Mr. Crowder said, "I'm glad to see a man doing his duty. We could use a little more of that in our shop, eh, Smalley? But you don't want to make a mountain out of a molehill. Little minds do that. We like to think big at CC&D. So I'll make you a proposition. You go back to New York, forget the whole business, and I'll keep you supplied with Towser Dog Biscuits for a year!" Mr. Crowder stepped back triumphantly to allow the full impact of his words.

"No go," Ryan said. "But I tell you what I'll do. Give this dog a fair shake. You put him in the water. If he acts like he wants to keep swimming, I'll go along with it. You just let the dog make up his own mind."

"By Godfrey," Mr. Crowder cried, "that's creative thinking for you! I'll buy that, sir! Smalley, bring out the dog!"

The assistant photographer and the copywriter carried the big shepherd to the float and paddled clear of the yacht. They lowered the animal into the water.

Without a moment's hesitation, the dog struck out for shore.

"That way! That way!" Mr. Crowder shouted, gesturing frantically in the direction of Manhattan.

The dog paid no attention. His eyes fixed on land, oblivious to the imprecations from Mr. Smalley, he paddled unswervingly to the dock.

"Does that settle it?" Ryan asked.

Mr. Crowder nodded glumly. The dog clambered ashore and shook himself, frolicking back and forth in the sun.

"Damned nonsense," Mr. Smalley muttered.

"Well, sir," Mr. Crowder said, "you've made your point. CC&D doesn't go back on its word."

"No hard feelings?" Ryan asked.

"No, no," Mr. Crowder said. "That's just the way the ball bounces. Well, Smalley, let's get back to the shop. Your boys had better come up with a new Towser campaign in one hell of a hurry, I'll tell you that."

As the agency people gathered on the deck, Ryan turned and started over the side.

"Wait a minute," Mr. Crowder called. "We give up on swimming the dog. But how about a human? Is that against the law?"

"Hell, no," Ryan said. "You can swim all you want."

Mr. Crowder seized his account executive by the shoulders. "Smalley, that's the answer. The old switcheroo. A *man* goes down the Hudson River! Listen, Smalley, do any of your boys know how to swim?"

Ryan continued down the gangplank. He did not wait to hear the answer.

23

Fifty Years in the Doghouse

In February, 1963, a Bronx livery stable went up in flames at about one o'clock, on a morning cast in solid ice. Somebody said you could hear the horses screaming for blocks away. Somebody else said the wiring was bad, probably. The old tinderboxes burn fast, the city won't even give out new licenses for them any more. The fire had already gone to three alarms by the time Colonel Rowan got there. Rousted out of bed by a phone call from the Manhattan Shelter, haphazardly bundled against the wind, Rowan was fully awake now. For a few minutes at the beginning, skidding the car along the white streets, he had been functioning mechanically and instinctively, after the manner of a soldier, drowsy but never caught entirely by surprise.

Victor Balluff and a couple of other Society agents reached the fire lines about the same time as Rowan. With the sirens still going, the men had to shout in each other's ears. The water had spread in slick puddles, the slush already beginning to freeze. Over most of the block, the flames turned sky and snow a delicate pink.

Nobody knew how many horses were trapped inside. The only information available—to anyone except a deaf man— was that there must be a lot of horses. To reach them, firemen started hacking through the walls. Balluff and the agents ran forward. Rowan noticed that Balluff wasn't wearing an overcoat and wondered, incongruously, whether he had forgotten it or felt more comfortable without it. Somebody said, "There must be a dozen." (Later, a count showed thirty horses.)

Rowan noticed that one of the Society's horse ambulances had rolled up through the slush. A little too close to the fire for comfort. Rowan called out, "Who the hell's driving in there?"

The window rolled down and a man leaned his head out. "What's the problem, Colonel?"

It was Ryan.

"Good God," Rowan said, "is that you?" Then he almost laughed, because Ryan gave him such a surprised look— much the same expression one uses in responding to any question whose answer is so obvious, in the category of a man with lather on his face and a razor in his hand being asked if he intends to shave.

Ryan climbed out of the ambulance. "Hell," he said with a grin, "There's horses here, aren't there?"

He headed for the burning stable. In the press of firemen, newspaper reporters, photographers, the white-haired Ryan moved on. He looked very tall, very steady, with the economical movements of a man who knows exactly what he is about.

Some horses were coming out. Five had already been burned to death. Another half dozen, scorched blind, their flesh seared, roasted on their bodies, were dying in agony. Merciful pistol shots sounded like sharp icicles breaking. A photographer ran up and took a flash picture. It was, after all, news.

Ryan led one animal at the end of a rope halter. Balluff had another one. At this point it was hard to tell which horses would survive. Even the ones able to walk might have had their lungs hopelessly burned. It was a fair bet that most would catch pneumonia.

Rowan found a telephone booth and called one of his old comrades-in-arms, now commander of a nearby military installation. Rowan wanted 50 blankets in a hurry. He got them by driving 20 miles in the stormy night.

Ryan started driving the surviving horses back to Manhattan. It was then approximately three in the morning. Fifteen horses lived.

In Manhattan, Ryan really got down to business. The veterinarians on emergency call had reported in. Ryan worked shoulder to shoulder with them, examining, treating; no one needed to tell him what to do. He had known for a long time. The vets were very good at their job. Beside Ryan, they also looked surprisingly young. There are not too many horses in New York now and it takes perhaps a split second to adjust to them. Ryan did not require that split second. His hands moved with practice and intuition. He had done it all before.

In one way or another. Horses. Dogs, cats, lions, elephants. The whole Arkful. For fifty years he had done this. He would keep on doing it. The only thing different was the ambulance.

On May 28, 1962, at the Society's Annual Meeting, President William Rockefeller presented a citation to William Michael Ryan. In part, the document read:

> For 50 years William Michael Ryan has diligently and with heart served the American Society for the Prevention of Cruelty to Animals and the animal population of New York State. . . . Tonight, we recognize this workaday humanitarian to whom animal lovers everywhere are indebted. William Ryan had devoted his life to the welfare of the entire animal kingdom, not because it was a duty, but because he is their friend.

Ryan is unique; to the extent that all things living are unique, individual, special in their own special ways. There are no exact duplicates among humans—or animals.

"When I first joined the Society," says William Mapel,

"Mr. Rockefeller told me: there's a great old fellow named Ryan down there. You ought to get to know him. You'll like him. He can probably tell you more about humane work than anybody in the place." Mapel adds, "I did. And he did."

Ryan is unique. Very seldom does a way with animals show itself so clearly in one person. Or, if it does show up, it may take a number of different forms.

Ryan is unique—but he is not alone.

Each year, the Society awards its Medal of Honor to an animal that has rescued a person and to a person who has performed a heroic service for an animal. Recently honored was a Seeing Eye dog that saved three humans from asphyxiation. A railroad brakeman received the medal for driving 120 miles, through deep snow in the middle of the night, to rescue a dog caught on a fence. Another honored was a volunteer fireman who rescued a kitten from a blaze and revived it with mouth-to-mouth respiration.

These are some of the reasons why Ryan is not alone.

"In truth," reads Ryan's citation, "the ASPCA honors itself in citing you for 50 years of devoted service, but even more so because you personify the meaning of the word 'care.' "

This may be the whole point. Ryan does what most humans would do—if we knew how. And, also, if we were willing to take the time, to go a little out of our way.

Some of us are overwhelmed at the task of giving a vitamin pill to a cat—justifiably, perhaps, depending on the cat. Very few of us would care to escort a wandering lion back to its cage. To this extent, Ryan is way ahead of us and we don't have much chance of catching up. Half a million animals in one lifetime isn't an easy record of match.

However, we can learn something that Ryan and the Society already know. Laws assure animals of protection—formally, officially, set down in black and white. But in the long run, the best protection is the human heart.

817
Alexander, L.

64- 022746

Fifty years in the doghouse.